DATE DUE

SCRIABIN

SCRIABIN
By ALFRED J. SWAN

GREENWOOD PRESS, PUBLISHERS
WESTPORT, CONNECTICUT

Originally published in 1923
by John Lane: The Bodley Head Ltd., London

First Greenwood Reprinting 1970

Library of Congress Catalogue Card Number 76-109859

SBN 8371-4350-0

Printed in the United States of America

PREFACE

THE present volume, while containing an outline of the outward events of Scriabin's career, is really a portrayal of the one supreme idea dominating the composer and an analysis of its musical reincarnation.

The book naturally subdivides into two parts: the biographical and the critical, each of which in its turn embraces a number of sections. The occasional symbolic headings of the latter seemed the only means of expressing compactly something very concrete and highly technical. In the second part every phase of Scriabin's activity is viewed from all its different angles, always reserving a central place for its purely musical peculiarities. The first part is based to a large extent upon facts given in Engel's biography of Scriabin (see vols. 4–5 of the "Musical Contemporary," Petrograd,1915–1916).

LONDON,
June, 1922.

CONTENTS

PART I

PART II

SCRIABIN

PART I

SCRIABIN

CHAPTER I

PARENTAGE AND CHILDHOOD

IT is but seldom that the appearance of a genius in some particular family cannot be accounted for. By following back a couple of generations one usually finds in certain members of the stock unmistakable signs of rare endowments that lurk in the dark and glimmer faintly. Then some unknown and mysterious influence, perhaps a fortunate influx of new blood, will fan the flame and suddenly bring the genius to light with supreme force.

The Scriabin family was not devoid of musical talent. Like so many noble Russian families with a preponderance of the military element, it had cultivated music for some generations in its old home in Moscow. Yet it was not until Nicolai Alexandrovich Scriabin, the second son of a major of the artillery, had fostered a bond with Lubov Petrovna Stchetinina, a pianist of a high order, that the stimulus to the appearance of genius was given. This happened probably early in 1871. Lubov Petrovna had then just finished the St. Petersburg conservatoire where she had studied under Leschetizki. Her playing and personality attracted the attention of the brothers Rubinstein, and the Grand Duchess Elena Pavlovna, a patron of music, condescended to take a kindly interest in her. Distinguished at her graduation by a gold medal, she was just about to start on her pianistic career in St. Petersburg and the provinces when her marriage to young Nicolai Alexandrovich Scriabin took place. They settled down in Saratov on the Volga and Nicolai Alexandrovich went into a lawyer's business. A programme of a concert given by Lubov Petrovna at that period, is extant. It includes the works of Liszt and Rubinstein. She could not have done much concert-playing, however, as she was expecting her first-born. It was about Christmas of the same year 1871 that the young couple went to Moscow to visit their family. Lubov Petrovna happened to catch a bad cold during that journey and arrived in Moscow ill and dejected. The same day a son—the future composer—was born to her. Strangely enough it was Christmas Day ; a fitting coincidence to which our great musical Messiah attached in after days a certain mystical importance.

Poor Lubov Petrovna ! It was not given

her to watch for long over her child. Predisposed as she was to consumption, the effects of her illness were more serious than could be anticipated. Less than a year later she had to be taken to a warmer climate. This, however, was of no avail, and in April 1873 she died at Arco in Southern Tyrol. A singular and tragic fulfilment of her grand mission in this world! Hers was a poetic appearance : perhaps not strictly beautiful, yet of a haunting charm. Her ash-coloured hair, black eyebrows, and the majestic calm of her features have a strange attraction. She imbued her son with the noblest traits of her artistic temperament, leaving it to him to develop them to vast proportions. Her portrait, painted by her brother, cast its mild glamour on the composer wherever he went or lived.

Remitting his son to the care of the grandmother and aunt, Nicolai Alexandrovich betook himself to serious studies. A man of undaunted energy and a somewhat cruel disposition, he was determined to shape his life in his own way. Taking honours in law and Oriental languages he entered the diplomatic service and became dragoman to the Russian embassy in Constantinople. The greater part of his life was spent in the Near East. Only every three years, when on leave, did he have a chance of seeing his boy. In 1880 he married again and had four children, all of them growing up to be totally unmusical. On his retirement Nicolai Alexandrovich settled down in Switzerland, where he lived quietly with his second family until his death in 1914. There was little affinity between him and his titanic son. However, they maintained friendly relations to the end, and on one occasion even paid a joint visit to Arco where Lubov Petrovna was buried.

And what of the boy himself? The absence of parental influence was of no moment in the plan of his life, since it was replaced a hundred-fold by the loving atmosphere of his grandparents' home. It was mainly Lubov Alexandrovna, Nicolai Alexandrovich's sister, who made his up-bringing the object of her life, and a debt of gratitude is due to her for having let his genius develop unhindered, unmolested by any artificial fetters, aided and furthered by her kindly concern and boundless attachment. She and her mother, young Sacha's (Alexander's) grandmother, took the most elaborate pains to direct the boy's inclinations into the right channels, to anticipate every possible turn of his character. The world of his childhood was soft and feminine, all his whims and fancies were rigid laws to the devoted women-folk. There was not a line of harshness about Sacha's infancy, and this left its lasting mark on his character : all through life he abhorred the graceless and uncouth, was shocked and grieved by any manifestation of vulgarity or obtrusive manners.

He was left to develop freely and on his own lines. There was no compulsion in anything. Playingly he learnt to read and write, playingly he strayed over the keyboard producing soft and delicate sounds with his elegant little fingers. He was never idle: the creative instinct whirled in him finding numberless forms of expression. One day he would carve out miniature pianos or embroider like his aunt. But no given pattern would please him. Whatever he did he wanted to do in his own individual way. Another day found him staging sombre tragedies in his own little theatre, declaiming and gesticulating. In his excitement he would make his heroes die long before the necessary five acts of the tragedy were over, and would then turn his bewildered look on his invariable audience (the aunt and the grand-mother) saying : " Auntie, there is no one left." With his fine ear for music he would reproduce on the piano whatever he happened to have heard. And his love for the latter instrument took the form of a strange, almost idolatrous obsession. He knew every little particle of its mechanism, kissed the instrument before going to bed, got strangely excited whenever the piano was moved from one place to another. He pedalled until there were holes in his little shoes, improvising before imaginary audiences. From his early years he evinced the same capacity for improvising as Chopin, and when it came to studying notation he found it tedious. In fact the first regular piano lessons he took from his aunt were rather unsuccessful, and the disconcerted Lubov Alexandrovna made off with the boy to Rubinstein himself to beg his advice in the matter of the child's musical training. "Don't force the boy ; let him follow his own impulse," was Rubinstein's counsel. And so Sacha was left in peace, his development flowing onward of its own accord.

CHAPTER II

YEARS OF APPRENTICESHIP

ALMOST in a wink passes a cloudless child-hood. No matter how reluctantly, but even our little hot-house flower has to face a more rigid system of education. He himself feels it too and begins to grow restless. His father's youngest brother, himself a mere little sixteen-year-old cadet, tells Sacha all about his life in the Moscow Military School, and Sacha is keen to follow the example of his uncle. After many entreaties he at last obtains permission to enter the institution and prepares for the examinations under the supervision of the ever-ready Lubov Alexandrovna. He has no difficulty in mastering all the needful subjects, and passes first out of seventy. In 1882, at the age of ten and a half, he is already clad in the wee military jacket with buttons of gold, and goes to live with another uncle of his, who is housemaster at the school. The feminine atmosphere of his child-hood is replaced by somewhat sterner, yet no less loving surroundings. Needless to say, all his vacations are spent with his aunt and grandmother, who take good care to move to a house not all too far from Sacha's school. At school his fine little individuality wins him many friends at once, and he even escapes the customary freshman thrashing. His classmates enjoy his brilliant and inventive little mind, and, above all, his power of producing magic sounds from the keyboard that seemed dead to them. Orders for all kinds of improvisations are sent in to him, and with great good nature and habitual readiness does Sacha cast the dormitory into an endless variety of moods. Again we are reminded of the youthful Chopin pacifying the noisy inmates of his father's *pension* by the heavenly sounds of his piano.

Sacha's popularity and the influence of his relatives built up for him an exceptional position at the military school. It was evident to anyone that the boy was not heading for a military career, and he was consequently exempted from the rigours of military discipline, drill, and in part even from special theoretical subjects. Here again his path was strewn with roses, and the atmosphere of a cadet school that often proves deadly to a sensitive child can be said to have had no harmful effects on Sacha's development. There may have been another reason for his preferential treatment by the school authorities : his health was not of the strongest. When he was twelve he nearly succumbed to a complication after measles, and for three successive summers he was taken to health resorts and made to undergo various cures. His studies at school progressed well, and he ranked among the best boys of his form. Soon, however, he was to embark on regular musical studies, and by-and-by they absorbed all his time and interest.

It was in the summer of 1883 that he first began to study piano-playing seriously. His teacher at that time was G. E. Konus, who was connected with the Moscow conservatoire. These lessons continued for about a year, and resulted in a firm determination on Sacha's part to enter the conservatoire at the very first opportunity. No obstacle was put in his way, though it meant for him the difficult task of combining twofold studies—those at the military school with those at the conservatoire. The private lessons with Konus were discontinued and the young improviser was made to undergo the stern regime of the old conservatoire professor, N. A. Zverev. For, alas, the stringent regulations of the senior course of pianoforte at the Moscow conservatoire were little sympathetic to mere high-flown improvisation. Zverev was eminently fitted for the task of dragging down to earth and bringing to his senses our young hero, who was speedily acquiring all the characteristics of a petted idol.

There was no nonsense about Zverev. He came of a wealthy family and had all his life regarded music as a pleasant pastime. Like so many Russian dilletanti, however, he contrived to acquire a real mastery of the piano, and when his large fortune was sufficiently squandered he was not inclined to refuse an invitation to a professorship at the Moscow conservatoire. A clever business-man in music, he also took in private boarders and drilled them relentlessly until he thought they were fit to go out into the world as pianists. But in spite of all his worldly qualities there must have been some divine spark in him, for he managed to turn out a certain number of pupils brilliant all round. At the time that Scriabin came to him his establishment included such future stars as Rachmaninov, Maximov, Pressman and others. Though he was not a boarder like the others, Scriabin invariably took part in all their musical doings and soon attracted universal awe and attention. His improvisations were now beginning to take a more definite turn, and it seems that a good many were affixed on paper in those days. Anyhow the boys regarded Scriabin as a composer of promise and enjoyed his Chopinesque little pieces. Not so Zverev, who minimized the significance of these early attempts of Scriabin and valued him solely as a coming great pianist. Many an evening was

devoted to music, the Zverev soirées beginning
generally after an opulent meal. All the pupils
had then to perform in turn before a distinguished
audience. Tchaikovski himself seems to have been
present at some of these gatherings. Scriabin
would shine in the execution of Schumann's
"Paganini" studies. But it was Chopin whom
he had taken to his heart, as can well be imagined.
He even used to sleep with the works of the
Polish master under his pillow. There was a
strange affinity between Scriabin and his prototype,
and a startling likeness in their way of approaching and handling the piano : all delicacy and
refinement.

A couple of years elapsed and Scriabin was
now well advanced on the high-road of piano-
playing. It was time to think of theoretical
studies. For this purpose no less a person than
Sergei Ivanovich Taneiev was approached. This
was probably in 1886, though dates are here not in
accord. A winter was spent at harmony exercises
and even counterpoint was attacked, Scriabin
applying himself with great diligence to the tasks
set him by the famous theoretician. Rapid progress
ensued, and it was thought that the time had now
come when Sacha could successfully join the conservatoire. The greatest care was taken to avoid
any gap in his knowledge, and in the summer of
1887 we see him going over harmony again with
Konus.

And, while academical requirements were thus
met on all sides, the trend of genius was making
itself felt apart from and in spite of them. A
small circle of friends grew up to encourage and
hail the young composer. In the home of one
Monigetti, a doctor by profession, Scriabin found
an atmosphere steeped in enthusiasm and admiration for his improvisations. And the general
Chopinesque background of the latter was being
markedly cut by sharper corners, the melodic
curve was becoming more fanciful, the harmonic
tissue closer and more intricate. Every new idea,
however rudimentary, was immediately demonstrated ; nay, even while in the process of com-
posing Scriabin disliked to be left alone. Many
a night would the grandmother's bedroom remain
empty, she herself lying down to rest on the sofa
while Sacha was working away at the piano. For
no sacrifice was too big if it tended to the care of
her beloved grandson.

It so happened that Scriabin did not actually
find himself within the walls of the Moscow
conservatoire until January 1888. This was
because he had joined the pianoforte class of
Safonov, and the latter was away all the autumn
on a concert tour. No one could be better suited
to become Scriabin's teacher and guide in piano-
playing than Safonov. This son of a rough
Cossack was the embodiment of ethereal grace

and delicacy in his treatment of the piano. He had studied under Louis Brassin and Leschetizki and had behind him several years of brilliant pedagogic experience. It is no exaggeration to say that his principles became focused in the playing of the young Scriabin—so akin to his own and yet so far surpassing it. With an unerring instinct Safonov discerned in Scriabin the signs of a pianistic genius and held him up to the emulation of the whole class. Scriabin's way of pedalling used to send him off in raptures. The instrument breathed and fluttered under Scriabin's fingers, and Safonov would listen forgetting all around him. It was on one such occasion that Safonov dozed off and woke up to the most ravishing sounds of the piano. Scriabin was still improvising. Jumping up Safonov asked him what he was playing. It was Scriabin's D flat major prelude (presumably from op. 11). " This," says Safonov, "remains one of the most delightful sensations of my life."

In 1889 Scriabin finished his course at the military school and could henceforth devote all his time to his music. His aunt and grandmother, with whom he continued living as of old, moved again, to be nearer Sacha's conservatoire. And under the kindly and appreciative supervision of Safonov, who, even, if he did not agree, let

Scriabin follow his own artistic impulse, the latter was making gigantic strides towards the consummation of his individuality. He used to appear at the conservatoire concerts playing Schumann's "Papillons," Chopin's mazurkas, and Bach's fugues. Wishing to be the first not only in interpretation but also in sheer technique, Scriabin attacked such stupendously difficult pieces as Balakirev's "Islamei" and Liszt's "Don Juan." It was then that he nearly ruined, Schumann-like, his whole pianistic career. His right hand was paralysed and the doctors had given it up. But with stoic perseverance Scriabin practised with the paralysed hand and brought it nearly to its former perfection. Practising the fingers of his right hand on whatever object they happened to lie, became a characteristic gesture with him all through later life. But a certain crampedness of the right hand in rapid octave passages fortissimo never disappeared entirely and was the source of much trouble during his concert tours even to the last years of his life. His studies under Safonov taking an auspicious turn, Scriabin was in the spring of 1891 awarded a pianist's diploma with the gold medal for piano-playing, an honour that was bestowed on his mother twenty years earlier. And, behold, Rubinstein likewise attended the departing pupils' concert. After Scriabin had played his own E major mazurka, the aged *maestro* promptly improvised variations upon it.

All did not go so well in the theoretical classes. Even Taneiev noted with grief a lack of interest in Scriabin for his admirable course in counterpoint. It was not that Scriabin was negligent. No one could possibly have the heart to be so, seeing how genuinely disappointed Taneiev was if any of his pupils failed to show the necessary application. But he evinced no love for contrapuntal studies, selected short themes for his exercises and was content to fulfil the bare requirements. However, for the two years that Scriabin was with Taneiev matters went passably. They became decidedly worse when he was transferred to the fugue class of Arenski. There was no love lost between master and pupil from the very beginning. Arenski lacked the Olympic grandeur of Taneiev; he was all but impartial in his strongly pronounced conservatism ; he was irritable and apt to be sarcastic and very unpleasant when he was crossed ; he failed to divine the powers of his titanic pupil. On the other hand the latter played a most unpardonable game with the feelings of his master. When told to write ten fugues during the summer vacation, he produced only one and entitled the second piece "fugue-nocturne." When expected to compose a scherzo, he appeared in class with an introduction to some Lithuanian opera. And when Rachmaninov, who was all the while his classmate, got permission to conclude the course in composition in a shorter period than usual, Scriabin with an astounding *naïveté* applied for a similar privilege. Arenski refused indignantly. Scriabin thereupon promptly left the conservatoire without a composer's diploma.

CHAPTER III

FIRST STEPS

THE wide world was before Scriabin, and not an easy one to get along in, with our young composer's highly strung sensibility and abnormal faith in his own powers. For as yet he was entirely unknown outside a small circle of intimate friends, and recognition would come but charily. Bitter disappointments were in store for him, and adverse criticism was not wanting even from well-disposed quarters. Thus Rimski-Korsakov speaks of him in his "Chronicle of my musical life" in the following terms : "In Moscow there has appeared a star of the first order—the somewhat mannered and presumptuous Scriabin."

At the outset of his pianistic career Scriabin was still living in Moscow with his aunt and grandmother. His right hand was still out of order ; he looked pale and delicate. At his concert appearances he was wont to appeal to the public, pointing to his weak hand. His associates in those days were of the easy-going, affable type, and Scriabin was often to be found playing billiards with them and otherwise enjoying himself. Among musical friends of that period E. K. Rosenov occupied a prominent place. To him the " Allegro appassionato " op. 4 was dedicated in manuscript (Scriabin never dedicated his compositions when printed). Rosenov was an excellent pianist and played Scriabin's works in his concerts. By-and-by Scriabin ventured to approach the publisher Jurgenson and showed him the mazurkas op. 3 and the nocturnes op. 5. Jurgenson did not refuse, but appeared cautious and extracted from Scriabin a certain commission. But no sooner were the things in print than they aroused the keen enthusiasm of some very influential people. Not the least among them was M. P. Beliaev. The debt that Russian music owes to this devoted art-lover is well known. What has endeared him above all to artists and critics was his unerring capacity to divine true genius in others. Just as in the young Glazunov he had discerned a maturing talent big enough to justify the opening of his publishing enterprise, so he instinctively divined signs of greatness in Scriabin's early works and proffered to the latter his aid and influence in a magnanimous and unreserved manner. He heard Scriabin play at a concert in St. Petersburg in the spring of 1894, and went into raptures over the studies op. 8. Not content with making the young pianist's acquaintance, he rushed to Moscow to introduce himself to the whole Scriabin family. Henceforth Beliaev's edition was always at Scriabin's disposal, and Beliaev was no miserly purchaser. The first works to appear under the familiar blue cover were the Sonata op. 6, the twelve studies op. 8, and the above-mentioned Allegro Appassionato. This was in 1895. Thus it came that Scriabin was received into the Beliaev circle. Not indeed as a regular member, for his journeys to St. Petersburg—the seat of the Beliaevists—were not all too frequent, but as a conspicuous and highly esteemed visitor. In Liadov, who was one of the mainstays of the Beliaev circle, Scriabin found a lifelong friend and up to a certain time an unqualified admirer. There was a great deal in the young Scriabin's music that was closely akin to the master of the miniature : careful workmanship, clearness and transparence of design, a Chopinesque atmosphere. And Liadov's enthusiasm knew no bounds ; as a member of the Beliaev jury he would handle the Scriabin manuscripts and even go to the trouble of correcting slight errors.

Beliaev did not stop short at publishing Scriabin's works and having him a regular guest at his house in St. Petersburg. In true Russian fashion he was wont to do the whole thing or not

do it at all.   He decided to present Scriabin to
the public, and organized an extensive tour for
him in Russia and abroad.   On this tour he
accompanied Scriabin in person, his fatherly
surveillance taking the curious form of following
him even on to the estrade, where Beliaev's huge
figure looked just like a case with the fragile
Scriabin taken out of it and placed by the piano.
The two spent the summer of 1895 in Switzerland on the Vierwaldstaetter lake.   It was here
that a number of the exquisite preludes op. 11
were composed.   Concerts were given in 1896
in Berlin, Brussels, Amsterdam, and Paris.   At
the first Paris concert Scriabin played some of the
preludes op. 11, the Allegro Appassionato, the
studies op. 8, some mazurkas, impromptus, and
the finale of the second sonata op. 19.   The press
received him well, a terse and very pertinent
criticism appearing in "La libre critique" (1896,
N. 4) : "an exquisite nature equally great as composer and pianist, an enlightened philosopher,
all nerve and a holy flame."   Scriabin liked Paris,
mixed in the musical world, and made a number
of friends.

On his return to Russia the concerts continued.
By this time many new works were completed.
The second sonata op. 19 was published in 1897,
and a third one was projected.   It was not, however, the later third sonata, and it was never

published. Rosenov says it was a fine work "in
the Gothic style," composed under the impression
of the ruins of a castle. Another important work
was the piano concerto op. 21, which was performed for the first time under Safonov at a
concert in Odessa in October 1897. All these
works began to attract the attention of eminent
pianists. Thus we find Scriabin among the composers performed by Joseph Hofmann ; and not
without reason, for the individuality of our author
was becoming more marked with every new opus.
In the beautiful second sonata he takes a forceful
leap out of the range of Chopin's influence. The
design of the first movement—a whimsical arabesque—and the impetus of the succeeding presto,
already reveal the later Scriabin " all nerve and a
holy flame."

It was about this time that Scriabin's marriage
to Vera Ivanovna Isakovich—a brilliant pianist
and a pupil of Professor Schloezer at the Moscow
conservatoire—took place. The young people
had met some some years before, and Scriabin
had been much impressed by Vera Ivanovna's
playing. Since then their ways had led them
apart, and Scriabin had bestowed his attention on
a young Italian lady for whom he wrote a song,
and later, in Paris, he was even engaged to a very
interesting and cultured young Russian. On his
return to Russia he met Vera Ivanovna again,

proposed to her, and the wedding took place in Nishni-Novgorod, where Vera Ivanovna's father lived. After a honeymoon in the Crimea the young couple went abroad for the winter (1897–98). During their stay in Paris they gave a joint concert of Scriabin's works, Scriabin playing the second sonata, and Vera Ivanovna the Allegro de Concert op. 18, together with a number of shorter works.

With the creation of a home of his own Scriabin's whole position in life underwent of necessity a decisive change. The petted darling of his aunt and grandmother, he had been devoid of all material cares, and used to spend the money that accrued to him from his concerts and compositions on travelling and other fancies. He had now to think of gaining a livelihood, and his earnings being uncertain he could do it only in a half-effectual way. Touchingly the staunch Beliaev came to his aid at the outset of his new life. He ordained an anonymous premium to be sent to Scriabin for his compositions. This premium became almost an annual occurrence and continued even after Beliaev's death, ranging between 500 and 1500 roubles. Besides this, Beliaev presented Scriabin with a piano, the complete works of Chopin, and in his fatherly tenderness even with a portmanteau for his prospective numerous journeys.

For the summer of 1898 the Scriabins returned to Russia and settled down at Maidanovo near Klin—some time also Tchaikovski's home. A happy family reunion took place, Scriabin's father and stepmother arriving to make the acquaintance of Vera Ivanovna. The crowning joy was the birth of Scriabin's eldest daughter Rimma. Scriabin himself was writing the third sonata for the piano (op. 23), the glorious apotheosis of his youthful ideals in music. The lovely A major theme in the finale became a favourite in the household, and would often be sung as a lullaby for the little Rimma. In the early autumn a further important event occurred. Safonov, Scriabin's former teacher, who had meanwhile become director of the Moscow conservatoire, invited him to the post of professor of the piano at his Alma Mater. The prospect of a permanent reliable income was too tempting to be set aside when a growing family had to be provided for ; and Scriabin accepted the offer, not, however, without grave misgivings.

CHAPTER IV

PROFESSORIAL DUTIES

SCRIABIN—the teacher—undoubtedly had his great moments : he gave interesting, original directions ; he required new life from every passage ; he imparted his individual technique of nerves to every little piece his pupils played. Spellbound would his class listen to his nervous and passionate rendering of Chopin and Schumann. He still lives in the recollections of his best pupils as a magician who opened up for them entirely new perspectives in music. Rarely did he give his pupils his own works for study ; yet in all they played it was their master's inflammatory personality that reigned supreme. In such inspired lessons Scriabin was eminently successful. Yet he failed completely in the systematic building up, the sustained pedagogical effort, the drudgery of everyday teaching. Confronted by some less gifted pupil slow in grasping his indications, Scriabin would be possessed by infinite boredom. It was these moments—and sometimes they were long hours—that he dreaded like poison and that made his professorship a dire burden to him. There was also the inevitable fact that his duties at the conservatoire kept him away from his creative outpourings—the only thing that had a real meaning for him. Thus it came that the years he spent at his Alma Mater were not the happiest of his life.

In his home he was also not too much at his ease. Vera Ivanovna spared no effort to make his home attractive for him. She stopped playing herself, preoccupied as she was by her domestic duties (two more girls and a boy were born in the succeeding years). But Scriabin preferred to ramble about in the company of friends, kept late hours, and often worked during the night. He was always lively, excited from performing his new works, demonstrating his new ideas on the piano even when they had hardly assumed a definite form. An elf, a soaring spirit—according to contemporary accounts of him—always kind, charming, with the softest of manners, he failed to impress one as the Titan of later days. Yet it was at this time that the overwhelming idea of his life was first nurtured and strengthened. It had its birth in the innermost depths of his being and remained individual to him regardless of all side influences. Scriabin's philosophy stripped of its musical reincarnation does not stand a comparison with other symmetrical and clear-cut systems. Scriabin had never been a serious student of philosophy, and the process of thought as such interested him but little. At all times of his life he raved about this or that philosopher without ever penetrating into his system as a whole. Thus he had his Nietzsche period and talked of writing an opera with the superartist for its hero. Then he became intimate with Prince Trubetskoi, a pupil of Vladimir Soloviov, and an exponent of the latter's deep and beautiful teaching. He cherished a great love for Trubetskoi, read his books, but was not shaken by his views. It was in the same way that at a later period he paid homage to theosophy. He picked out from a number of philosophical systems traits that seemed to echo his own ideas and used the former to make the latter more convincing. The truth was then that all his philosophy emanated from the nature of his music and stimulated him to fresh designs.

In the year after the composition of the third sonata (1899) he turned for the first time to the orchestra and wrote the delicate little Reverie op. 24. The next year saw the production of his first symphony op. 26. Safonov was enthusiastic about these two works and, as conductor of the Moscow symphony concerts, produced them both with all the care that he was capable of.* The press was very deferential and attentive,

* Reverie, March 12, 1899 ; 1st Symphony, March 16, 1901.

and welcomed the first orchestral works of a composer who had hitherto devoted himself exclusively to the piano. In the finale of the symphony Scriabin attempted to give vent to his ideas of universal—social, religious and philosophical—unity. These ideas were beginning to dominate him and formed the germ of his later Mystery. But as yet they were devoid of any trace of mysticism. He introduced a chorus to sing a hymn of praise to art, the eternal bond of all peoples and races. He was, however, only groping his way in a new sphere and failed to find adequate means of expression : this finale is vastly inferior to the other unpretentious parts of the symphony.

Scriabin's struggle for a spiritual outlook was accompanied by rapid strides towards a complete emancipation from his early musical influences. The last tribute to Chopin was paid in the 9 mazurkas op. 25, while Wagner received his due in the rather heavily scored second symphony op. 29. Scriabin's contact with Wagner was, however, only an outward one. He knew Wagner's operas and was fond of them, but always criticized Wagner's lack of form. A storm of controversy swept over Moscow at that time in connection with R. Strauss's works. Scriabin disliked Strauss, yet found some of his methods interesting. He was speedily approaching the stage of greater or lesser indifference to all music ; he was too much preoccupied by his own development. Before he tore off all fetters he was to undergo another side influence—that of Liszt, whose overwhelming artistic personality always attracted him greatly. This influence is felt already in parts of the second symphony (slow movement) and in the works for the piano immediately following it. The second symphony was performed for the first time under Safonov on March 21, 1903, while the year before a concert had been arranged devoted entirely to the works of Scriabin. All these events were but moderately successful. The large public was partly indifferent, partly even hostile—as at the first performance of the second symphony, when loud hisses were mixed with applause. A whole decade was to pass before Scriabin was powerful enough to command universal awe and the unbounded admiration of crowds of progressive concert-goers and critics.

After five years in Moscow, Scriabin grew so weary of his professorial duties that he definitely decided to relinquish his post. A turbulent creative wave was seething in him and leaving no room for any other thought or occupation but composition. Vast prospects were being formed, new horizons unveiled. Scriabin was now determined to earn a sufficiently large sum of money to enable him to spend the winter in Switzerland in the realization of these projects. Opus after opus was sent to the press, the superb fourth sonata op. 30, the two poems op. 32, a score or so of preludes, the Tragic and Satanic poems (op. 34 and 36). The summer of 1903 was spent in a breathless hurry, preparations were made for the coming journey, an offer of a professorship at the Vienna conservatoire (made to Scriabin on hearing of his resignation in Moscow) was wittingly declined. Yet with all resources taxed to their utmost, the eleventh hour revealed the impossibility of going, from purely financial considerations. Not even the Beliaev premiums were sufficient. Here a *deus ex machina* stepped in, in the person of a wealthy pupil, M. K. Morozova, who assigned to Scriabin an annual income of 2400 roubles (about £250) for an indefinite period. Overjoyed, the family set out on their journey (February 29, 1904).

CHAPTER V

Voluntary Exile

IN those days Scriabin had a very high opinion
of Switzerland and its freedom-loving
people, and regarded it as a suitable country
for the furtherance of his new ideas. In later
years he was somewhat shaken in this belief and
transferred his sympathies to other lands.

The family settled down in Vésenaz on Lake
Geneva. Scriabin was possessed of a tumultuous
longing for a complete spiritual transformation of
humankind. He dreamed of a synthesis of all
arts, philosophy and religion—a new gospel to
take the place of the old. He talked exube-
rantly to his friends, who comprised a great
variety of folk in all stations of society. Thus,
there was a fisherman by the name of Otto with
whom Scriabin was very intimate. They were in
the habit of spending their evenings in a little
café over a glass of beer, Scriabin talking and
preaching unremittently, thundering at the exist-
ing order and propagating his Utopian ideas.
There was sometimes quite a crowd listening to
all his effusions. How many were there among

these simple burghers who understood the Russian idealist ready to embrace the whole universe ? But Scriabin cared little. This was only a natural outlet for his colossal agitation which was musically moulding itself into the monumental third symphony, one of the stepping-stones in his sweeping course towards the Mystery.

The third symphony, or the Divine Poem, as it was called, was copied out by Vera Ivanovna and sent to the press in November 1904. To accelerate the public performance of this music—"such as had never before been written"—a scheme was devised by which' Arthur Nikisch was persuaded to conduct it at the Théâtre Châtelet in Paris in the following spring. Nikisch's inducement being not wholly disinterested, M. K. Morozova's financial help was resorted to and the symphony was heard for the first time on May 29, 1905. In that year Russia's international prestige had suffered a severe blow from the Japanese. The Russian ambassador, who was present at the concert, witnessed the considerable success of Scriabin's wonderful work and uttered the words : "In war we suffer defeat, but in art we are triumphant." Awaiting this happy event in his life, Scriabin was staying in Paris while his family continued living in Vésenaz. All this last year abroad his relations to Vera Ivanovna were undergoing a radical change. To discourse on the reasons of the alienation that took place between them must needs be idle talk. Some years ago in Moscow Scriabin had met a young girl— Tatiana Feodorovna Schloezer—whose very being seemed to reflect the minutest turn of his mind, to throb at the flight of his inspiration, to divine, as only a woman can divine, the most cherished treasures of his genius. From the moment they met Scriabin felt himself linked to her irrevocably. She herself tells the story of her early infatuation for Scriabin and his music. Ever since she was about fourteen (she was born in 1883) she had played the works of Scriabin and had been enthusiastic about them together with her elder brother, Boris Feodorovich Schloezer—now a well-known philosopher and writer on music. In the Caucasus she had heard the pianist Buyukli play the third sonata and this had been the strongest impression of her youth. Determined to meet the composer, she went to Moscow and began to take lessons from Scriabin. But, feeling how insignificant her own musical personality was beside that of her master, she just let it dwindle away, and in her very absorption in Scriabin's genius became a mighty stimulus to its powerful progress. There was now no parting of their ways. Yet the responsibility was grave and, maybe, they tried to postpone the critical moment. Writing from Switzerland to Boris

Feodorovich Schloezer Scriabin suggested that his sister should come out to live near Vésenaz " for the sake of her health." So Tatiana Feodorovna came soon and settled in Belle-Rive, twenty minutes' journey from Vésenaz. When Scriabin went to Paris she followed him there, and after the performance of the Divine Poem the inevitable happened : they decided to consummate their longing for each other and separate no more.

The noble and courageous attitude of Vera Ivanovna during this time of crisis remains a token of her profound respect for Scriabin's artistic personality. Anticipating the change that was to come, Scriabin prepared Vera Ivanovna for a life independent of him. He studied with her his own works (up to op. 42) and oftentimes intimated to her that he might have to leave her. Their correspondence continued while he was in Paris and lasted as long as January 1906. They were destined to meet once more on the occasion of the death of their eldest daughter, Rimma : Scriabin wept bitterly over the untimely grave. In the autumn of 1905 Safonov invited Vera Ivanovna to a professorship of the piano at the Moscow conservatoire, and in March 1906 she began the series of concerts devoted to the works of Scriabin. These concerts she continued for many years to come.

The summer of 1905 found Tatiana Feodo-

D

rovna and Scriabin in Boliasco on the Italian Riviera. Basking in the hot sun, fanned by the breeze from the azure sea, amidst a lovely orange grove, Scriabin let his genius soar into unfathomable regions. The satisfaction of his desire to be constantly near the woman who was prepared to follow him " to the edge of the limitless," opened new springs of overflowing inspiration. This was the time of the conception of the Poem of Ecstasy, the song of struggle victorious and triumphant. He used to play fragments of it to his numerous friends on a dreadful instrument borrowed from a neighbouring café. A memorable little colony of Russian emigrants was assembled at Boliasco, all eagerly watching the tide of events in their native land on the eve of the first great convulsion (1905). There was G. A. Plekhanov, the socialist leader, who used to heckle Scriabin about his mysticism and the paramount place in his universe assigned to the individual. There was Scriabin's former pupil, M. S. Lunz, and her husband Dr. Lunz, mostly realists engaged in an actual political struggle. Scriabin must have been a strange contrasting figure in their midst, playing to them his Valse op. 38 and explaining it as a beautiful evanescent dream. Not wishing to remain behind the others, he, too, read books on socialism. But other books interested him far more. He had just then been initiated into the depths of theosophy, and India began to form the object of his secret fancies. Of the Russian poets, Tutchev, Balmont, and Viacheslav Ivanov were very dear to him and kindled his desire to precipitate the Mystery, the ultimate goal of all his defiant ventures in art.

Ten bright months were gone almost in a wink, and in February 1906 the Scriabins moved to Geneva. A time of hardship was before them. Beliaev's death in 1903 caused certain changes in the administration of his publishing house, and, while in Boliasco, Scriabin received an intimation that his salary would be reduced by one-half owing to unforeseen circumstances. Hurt by the official tone of the letter, he wrote back rejecting the terms of his contract with the Beliaev firm. The result was disastrous. All negotiations with other firms failed, Zimmermann in Leipzig actually offering him to write popular waltzes at the rate of twenty-five roubles each, instead of the preludes (op. 48) that he had sent in. Scriabin was without editor. A concert given in Geneva in June 1906 did not solve the financial difficulties. Just at this embarrassing juncture Tatiana Feodorovna's father sent him an advertisement by Modest Altschuler in New York inviting Russian composers to send in their orchestral scores for performance in America. Scriabin wrote to Altschuler, who had been his contemporary at the

Moscow conservatoire, and in reply received an offer to come over to New York with scores and all. Altschuler's terms were modest, but on the whole acceptable to Scriabin in his unexpected misfortune. And so he embarked on what proved to be a most ill-advised journey. He had to leave Tatiana Feodorovna and their one-year-old daughter at Amsterdam and sailed alone after two farewell concerts in Brussels (November 1906).

Altschuler was genuinely interested in Scriabin, and it was mainly thanks to him and to Safonov, who had retired from his directorship in Moscow and was enjoying a great popularity in New York, that Scriabin's symphonies achieved a considerable success. There were a few memorable concerts in Carnegie Hall (December 1–20). Altschuler and Safonov conducted and Scriabin was recalled many times. Then he went on tour to Chicago and Cincinnati, appearing as a pianist and playing his own works only. Safonov's attitude towards Scriabin was, however, no longer the same as of old. The change in him was due first of all to Scriabin's musical evolution which was alien to the conservative Safonov, and not in a small degree to the rupture with Vera Ivanovna.

In private New York circles Scriabin also aroused very considerable interest. He evidently contemplated a prolonged stay in America and was anxious for Tatiana Feodorovna to come over and bring with her the still unfinished score of the Poem of Ecstasy. She arrived in January 1907. Her coming changed the whole outlook. Safonov stupidly turned round and became very stiff, seeing in Tatiana Feodorovna the cause of Scriabin's "musical and moral downfall." Safonov's new manner acquired publicity and there might have resulted a similar scandal as in the case of Maxim Gorki. Fortunately Altschuler warned the Scriabins in time, and they at least escaped the humiliation of a rough and ready treatment by unscrupulous authorities. However, it was bad enough for them. Impending engagements cancelled, contracts broken, they had hardly enough to defray the expenses of the homeward journey, and arrived in Paris with thirty francs in their pocket. March 1907 was a dark month in Scriabin's life.

A distinguished company of Russian musicians was assembling in Paris at the time of the Scriabins' arrival. A great musical event—the Diaghilev concerts—was forthcoming in May. At these concerts the Scriabin symphonies were to be performed along with other masterpieces of Russian music. And good friends of olden days were not lacking. Scriabin met the Rimski-Korsakov family, Glazunov, Rachmaninov and others. Rimski-Korsakov's interest in Scriabin's development had not diminished. Many an evening was spent in the Café de la Paix in talks about the Mystery, and many points in common were discovered. Not the least was a similar tendency to associate harmonies with colours, though Rimski's perception of the colour scale did not always coincide with Scriabin's. Fragments of the Poem of Ecstasy were demonstrated with the aid of Tatiana Feodorovna, but it found little favour with the listeners. The pianoforte pieces were on the other hand eliciting unrestrained admiration. Through Rimski a reconciliation with the Beliaev firm took place : the old terms were renewed and the publication of the Poem of Ecstasy was settled. The general tenor of this short sojourn in Paris was a great consolation to Scriabin after the hard times through which he had just passed. The feeling grew with him that he still possessed powerful friends in Russia who would support him if he ever wished to return home. With a double vigour he set about to finish the work that had swayed his emotions since Boliasco. The summer 1907 was spent in Switzerland, in Beatenberg. It was a peculiarity of Scriabin's to talk of conceived works as if their completion was a question of days only. So it was with the Poem of Ecstasy. For it was late autumn of the same year, and the Scriabins had already moved to Lausanne, before it was actually sent to print.

For three weeks Scriabin and Tatiana Feodorovna slept only three to five hours daily to get it into shape and it appeared in January 1908, just before the birth of their son Julian.

But while Scriabin's great orchestral works were left to mature in his mind, their offshoots in the shape of pianoforte sonatas and miniature works sprang up almost miraculously, products of a flash of inspiration. Thus the fifth sonata, this deed of wondrous magic, was composed in the course of several days just as Scriabin's mind was most intent on the Poem of Ecstasy. This fifth sonata (op. 53) together with the three pieces op. 52 became the victims of a strange and sudden commercial venture by which Scriabin hoped to improve his still tottering finances. Not content with Beliaev's way of bringing out his compositions, Scriabin decided to publish the piano works himself and got into touch with the Paris firm Enoch who were to hold them in stock. The latter were not in the least interested in Scriabin and made no attempt at advertising. After several months the net profit was a few francs of which Scriabin was very proud, but which could hardly be called a business success. At this moment a saviour appeared in the person of S. A. Kussevitski, who had just founded the new Russian Music Edition in Berlin. Kussevitski was anxious to obtain Scriabin's works for his publishing enterprise. He hurried to Lausanne in the spring of 1908 and very soon he and Scriabin were good friends. He offered to pay Scriabin 5000 roubles per annum, in return for which Scriabin would give him all his smaller compositions and the Mystery when completed. Incidentally he bought from Enoch the two stray opus numbers which were the first to appear in Kussevitski's edition.

Happier financial prospects seemed to open before Scriabin. He rejoiced in the company of friends and admirers. His father arrived from Turkey to make the acquaintance of Tatiana Feodorovna. Boris Feodorovich Schloezer and his wife were also Scriabin's guests for a time. Pianists came to pay homage to him and study the interpretation of his works. Thus the pianist Meichik took with him to Russia the fifth sonata, and revealed it there to the astounded public whose interest in Scriabin was growing from day to day. The crowning excitement came in the nature of an invitation from the Imperial Russian Music Society in Moscow. M. K. Morozova— Scriabin's staunch supporter, and now a director of the above society—could not forgo an opportunity of having the prophet come back to his own country. A mass of emotions was stirred in Scriabin by this long-aspired honour which showed him that his great evolution was being closely watched at home. Great was the temptation to accept and go at once. But family reasons prevailed and the homeward journey was postponed till next year (1909). Meanwhile three concerts had been given in Lausanne in November 1907, and April and July 1908 ; the month of August was pleasantly passed with the Kussevitskis at Biarritz, where a bust of Scriabin was made by the sculptor Sudbinin. In the autumn the family, together with Tatiana Feodorovna's mother, settled down in Brussels. This sojourn in Brussels is most noted for the further stimulus it gave to Scriabin's philosophy. The Mystery idea became more minutely crystallized. A spirited and enthusiastic little circle of friends was wont to assemble at Scriabin's abode, 45 Rue de la Reforme, discussing questions of art and theosophy and arguing till the small hours. There were the artist Delville, who was later to design the cover of the Poem of Fire, Emile Cygogne, a professor of elocution, a man with a Hellenic soul so different from and yet so sympathetic to Scriabin's Eastern mysticism. In all his intercourse with others Scriabin was at once confiding and suspicious. Excessive admiration of his later works rendered him cautious until he was convinced of the sincerity of the admirer. But if he came to like some one he almost invariably began to ascribe to him his own ideas. He argued aggressively and heaped scorn and ridicule on many an artist and composer. Tchai-kovski fared particularly ill in these discussions.

Soon preparations were started for the coming journey to Moscow—so sweet and yet so hazardous. By the end of 1908 the Scriabins were in Berlin, and in January 1909 "mother Moscow" received back her titanic son.

CHAPTER VII

HOME ONCE MORE

FIVE long years had elapsed since Scriabin left Russia. His musical evolution had made gigantic strides, placing him in the front rank of daring innovators. His music had ceased to be intelligible to many an enthusiastic admirer of his earlier style. Thus Liadov, once so sympathetic, failed to see in the works of the Divine Poem period anything but " horrible monsters." Glazunov and the Moscow critic, Kashkin, went a step further, seeing the climax of Scriabin's development in the Divine Poem, but declaring themselves unable to follow into the regions of the Poem of Ecstasy. How would these two monumental works be received by the Russian public ?

There were also private reasons for anxiety arising out of Scriabin's changed family relations. But his aunt and grandmother welcomed their darling with all of their old loving ardour, and the concert, under the direction of E. A. Cooper, including the Divine Poem, the fifth sonata and the Poem of Ecstasy, turned out a victory beyond all expectation (February 21, 1909). The excitement of music lovers was universal. An article by B. F. Schloezer heralded the approach of this momentous concert, and six rehearsals were required to overcome the stupefaction of the orchestra. Shortly before this, the Poem of Ecstasy was performed in St. Petersburg, but there the praise was not quite so unanimous. Scriabin attended the performance, met Liadov and other friends of younger days. He also made the acquaintance of the poet Viacheslav Ivanov, whose cosmic conception, as revealed in his poetry, he had long regarded as closely akin to his own. A lifelong friendship grew up between the two artists.

Torrents of talk, keen interest, wide dissension, and a grand enthusiasm were evoked by Scriabin's appearance in Russian musical circles. Yet this time he had not come to stay. He journeyed back to Brussels, but not without a feeling of regret. Why continue living in voluntary exile when his native country—in those days one of the most advanced and cultured in every branch of art and thought—had shown signs of deep appreciation?

The idea of the Poem of Fire (Prometheus) was already burning in him, and he contemplated new and daring conquests. All through 1909 he was working at what was destined to become

his last orchestral utterance. " Prometheus " was
acquiring shape and substance in the mighty grip
of the composer. By the beginning of the
following year the Scriabins were back in Moscow,
this time for good. All the old friendships were
renewed and many more formed, as with Nicolai
Medtner—already a prominent figure in musical
Moscow. Scriabin was so full of the Poem of
Fire, and, as was customary with him, talked so
much of its completion in the nearest future, that
Kussevitski actually announced an extra concert
in the spring of 1910 that was to bring this new
work and also a series of " Symphonic dances."
The latter existed in Scriabin's head only. There
is no indication of their ever having been put on
paper. But even the Poem of Fire was not
nearly ready for the concert, and Kussevitski had
to perform the Poem of Ecstasy instead of it.
This was, however, a very different performance
from the one that had taken place a year ago.
Kussevitski had now formed his own orchestra,
which gave him ample opportunity to develop
his great gifts as conductor. The works of
Scriabin, in their harmonic complexity, possessed a
special attraction for him. He worked hard, and
the result was a truly wonderful interpretation of
the Poem of Ecstasy, with the minutest detail
brought out to supreme efficacy. The success
with the public was complete. Soon after this

Kussevitski organized a tour of the Volga towns
with his orchestra. Scriabin was invited to take
part in it. A steamer was chartered, a special
Bechstein piano prepared for Scriabin, and beginning April 21, 1910, nineteen concerts were given
in eleven towns. Nearly everywhere Scriabin
played his early pianoforte concerto, and his
symphonic works occupied a prominent place in
Kussevitski's programmes. This tour diverted
Scriabin's attention from the Poem of Fire, and
he did not finish it till late in the summer of
1910 while living on an estate near Moscow.

The approach of the day of its first performance—March 2, 1911—was accompanied by an
unheard-of excitement in the musical and artistic
world. Every one acquainted with the manuscript score realized the colossal grandeur and
significance of the work, marking a new shift of
Scriabin's harmonic scheme, and revealing a wealth
of music of the purest and most dazzling beauty.
To his tonal scales Scriabin added a colour scale
that was played on a new instrument—the Clavier
à lumière. The construction of this instrument,
however, entailed such difficulties that it was
finally decided to give the work without it.
Kussevitski entered heart and soul into the study
of the poem and arranged for nine orchestral
rehearsals. The performance—an exceedingly
fine one—electrified all Moscow. The public

was aghast. Two hostile camps sprang up and the critics began to wage a regular war in the press. Fine articles in support and acclamation of the work appeared from the pen of O. O. von Riesemann, B. F. Schloezer, and Leonid Sabaneiev. But violent attacks were not wanting, as usual. Musical history has supplied us with instance after instance of similar scuffles of opinion produced by events of the first magnitude. Suffice it to recall Monteverde's Madrigali, Beethoven's seventh symphony, Moussorgski's "Boris Godunov," and Debussy's "A l'après midi d'un faune." The two latter have become classics before our very eyes, and the ten years that have passed since the first performance of "Prometheus" have pacified and converted some of the most indignant critics (*e.g.* the St. Petersburg critic Victor Kolomitsev). Recent presentations of Scriabin's orchestral masterpiece have attracted huge audiences, and the time is not far distant when it will secure its place beside the above pillars of music.

Soon after the first performance of "Prometheus" the friendship between Scriabin and Kussevitski suffered an eclipse. Two strong personalities, they brought pressure to bear on each other and very indiscriminately obstructed each other's freedom of action. The result was a lamentable rupture which, however, did not prevent Kussevitski from giving Scriabin's works in his numerous concerts. Scriabin's circle in Moscow now included the acute and eminently learned Leonid Sabaneiev, the author of a book on Scriabin. Sabaneiev became Scriabin's adviser in matters connected with acoustics and musical science. He encouraged Scriabin on the new harmonic path that was inevitably leading the composer to the boundaries of the tempered system towards ultra-chromaticism. B. F. Schloezer, on the other hand, was furnishing the backbone to Scriabin's philosophic ideas. Besides these two men the poets V. Ivanov and J. K. Baltrushaitis were Scriabin's constant and faithful counsellors. They were not unaware of the great poetic significance of the Mystery that was to embrace all the arts, and helped Scriabin with the invention of its language of sighs and ejaculations. And by the time the Poem of Fire was completed, the thought of the coming cataclysm and his Mystery had obtained full possession of Scriabin. With this one idea in mind the post-Promethean piano sonatas were conceived in the summer of 1911, which he spent in Kashira, a village on the border of the Moscow and Tula provinces. It was, however, not till 1912-13 that these offshoots from the Mystery were written down. This was due partly to Scriabin's preoccupation with the Mystery itself, and partly to the extensive concert tours that are an important feature

of Scriabin's last years. He had completely overcome his former dislike of public appearances.
Festal surroundings, an atmosphere of worship
and admiration, became a prime necessity to him.
Yet every time he was accorded a warm reception,
he was as if surprised, felt proud of it, and liked
to talk about it to his friends. In the season
1911–12 many provincial towns were visited,
Scriabin playing mostly his earlier works. Tatiana
Feodorovna accompanied him almost without
exception. In Moscow he played that season
with Rachmaninov as a conductor, while in St.
Petersburg it was A. Siloti who henceforth in his
concerts became an ardent propagandist of
Scriabin's music. No concert cycle was now
regarded as complete that did not bring at least
one or two works of Scriabin. Thus St. Petersburg heard " Prometheus " twice that season,
under Siloti and under Kussevitski, and though
Siloti lacked Kussevitski's wonderful grip and
elaboration of the detail, his rendering nevertheless exhibited many fine qualities. Siloti, who
had only recently become a convert to Scriabin's
music, threw himself heart and soul into the task
of making it known at home and abroad. In the
autumn of 1912 he inaugurated for Scriabin a
tour in Holland which turned out a triumphal
passing for the composer. On Oct. 27, 1912,
the Poem of Fire was performed in Amsterdam

E

with Mengelberg conducting, and made a deep
impression on the audience. The summer previous
to this tour Scriabin spent in Beatenberg (Switzerland) and finished there his sixth sonata for the
piano (op. 62). The seventh sonata—Scriabin's
favourite " white mass "—appeared a short while
before and had been played by him at a late
spring concert in St. Petersburg. The baffling,
intoxicating effect of this concert—April 8, 1912
—bringing for the first time not only the seventh
sonata but also " Masques " and " Etrangeté,"
will not easily be forgotten by those who were
present. All these works were the last to appear
in Kussevitski's edition. By the instrumentality
of Siloti Scriabin got in touch with Jurgenson,
the publisher, who had exacted a rigorous commission from him some twenty years ago. This
same Jurgenson now offered to pay him 6000
roubles yearly besides a royalty for the copyright
of his works ! In November 1912 the Scriabins
settled down in the Great Nicolo-Peskovski Lane
in Moscow. This was to be his last abode.

Times had changed. Round his home, once
so unattractive to him, Scriabin's whole life and
thoughts now began to centre. It was here that
the festal atmosphere of the concert room found
it natural culmination. Friends assembled, a
lively intercourse and exchange of ideas on art
and music flourished, card games and chess also

received their due, food and drink were never removed from the table, the samovar kept boiling till late at night. Scriabin was very particular about outward things, liked good clothes, old furniture, precious china. He was fastidious to an almost unnatural degree about the physical and sanitary side of his person. To prevent his hair from falling out, hair washing was a complicated procedure ; never did he dare to use a brush or comb that was not his own, walked bareheaded, always wore gloves, and dreaded infection like poison. It was as if he had a forewarning about the nature of his last illness. His attitude towards people was greatly modified. His former expansivity and communicativeness had well-nigh disappeared. He was always on his guard, yet polite and soft as usual. Behind his charm of manner there was, however, an extreme self-appreciation. He was impatient of contradiction and lent an ear to advice and criticism from such people only whose fundamental sympathy with his ideas was beyond doubt. To this group of people belonged, besides Sabaneiev and the poets Baltrushaitis and Ivanov, Doctor Bogorodski, N. S. Jiliaev, the Princes Gagarin and Trubetskoi, and the artist Sperling who presented him with a picture of an Eastern sage. This was the little circle that witnessed the growth of the Mystery, discussed the possibilities of its near realization, speculated on the extinction of our civilization and its replacement by a new one emanating from the East. It was to these men that Scriabin demonstrated also the musical incarnation of his thoughts, sometimes in the form of one poignant harmony only. For he still spoke of his compositions as nearly finished when they barely existed in his head, and started writing them down at once, leaving a precise number of bars to be filled in later. This formal preciseness was always very strong in Scriabin, and maintained itself in the face of the most turbulent harmonic innovations. Towards his own compositions he was very exacting and paid the minutest attention to matters of orthography, unimportant as this might seem in his synthetic harmonies. His latest work he invariably spoke of as his best, and was not at all interested in arrangements of older works : thus he never even glanced at L. Konus' reduction for the piano of his Divine Poem and Poem of Ecstasy. Towards other composers his interest was also on the wane, yet he used to express certain opinions about the Russian national school of which he quaintly imagined himself a distinguished member. He valued Moussorgski for his great natural genius, and Rimski-Korsakov for his refinement and careful workmanship. Of the Germans, Wagner alone moved him to the last ; Bach he considered dry, yet superior to Beethoven, whose forms only he admired.

Scriabin's fame was spreading steadily both at home and abroad. The next season—1912-13—saw the production of the Poem of Fire in London under Sir Henry Wood. The poem was given twice in one concert—a device invented by Siloti—so as to facilitate its comprehension by the public, and created a deep stir. The summer of 1913 Scriabin spent on the river Oka. He was resting from the strain of the winter months in which the three last sonatas—the eighth, the ninth, and the tenth—grand, immortal works, the radiant summit of Scriabin's harmonic evolution, were affixed on paper. Baltrushaitis was living near in the country, and Sabaneiev and others were frequent visitors.

The distance separating Scriabin from the realization of his life—the Mystery—was swiftly diminishing.

A new concert tour was embarked upon in the autumn and winter, and finally in February 1914 Scriabin went to England. His fame had preceded him there. As far back as 1909 Kussevitski had conducted in London his first symphony, and in 1910, introducing the Poem of Ecstasy, the same conductor spoke memorable words to the orchestra about the great importance of the work in the history of music, words that had

taken deep root in the hearts of the executants.
So when Scriabin appeared in person, and the
Poem of Fire was given again under Sir Henry
Wood, the applause was prodigious, and the press
unanimous in its estimation of the work. Scriabin's piano recitals were equally successful, and
the composer was enthralled by his reception.
He spoke of England in terms of the highest
admiration, placing her in the vanguard of
humanity on account of her moral worth and high
type of civilization. He rejoiced over the growing friendship between her and Russia, and in his
thoughts even bestowed on her the loftiest distinction that he was capable of: after India, he said,
England was the most suitable place for the
service of the Mystery. Switzerland had long
ago fallen into disgrace with him. He himself
made a lasting impression on the London musical
world by the charm and unpretentiousness of his
demeanour. New friendships were formed, among
others with Professor Myers of Cambridge, who
from a physicist's point of view regarded Scriabin's harmonic inventions as a stroke of genius
and invited him to Cambridge. The week-end
at the ancient university thrilled Scriabin. An
increasing excitement was taking possession of
him. He was making plans for a trip to India,
bought a tropical hat, spoke to practical men
about the cost of the construction of a temple in

India wherein the mysterious service might be held. On his return to Russia the last offshoots from the Mystery were thrust upon an astonished musical world in the shape of his last ten works for the piano—the Poems op. 71, Vers la Flamme, the two dances op. 73 and the five preludes op. 74.

Henceforth he was absorbed in his gigantic idea. In Podolsk, near Moscow, in the summer of 1914 he wrote with a great concentration of powers the poetic text to the Initial Act, a sort of prologue to the Mystery. Trembling and excited he proffered this text to the judgment of his two poet-friends Baltrushaitis and Ivanov. Wonder-stricken and amazed they hailed it as a portion of a stupendous work of art and religion. Scriabin waked all night in a boundless excitement making new daring projects. Then the war broke out, and Scriabin embraced it enthusiastically. The beginning of the sweeping cataclysm seemed near at hand. In the autumn, with the advent of the wounded, he was roused to the relief of suffering, and gave big concerts in aid of various war-time organizations, finding again little time for work. These concerts had latterly become real festivals for the great bulk of concert-goers and intellectuals. Seats would be obtained with the utmost difficulty, after many hours of "standing in a row." Scriabin's appearance would be greeted

with the exuberance of the masses acclaiming a
prophet and leader. The nervous strain of the
wizard at the piano would affect the last person
in the concert-hall, causing such an intensity of
perception in all, as to break out into a tumultuous
uproar at the end of every little prelude or poem.
The number of encores would sometimes exceed
the length of the programme, the crowd thronging
round the estrade and the composer in an irresistible desire to catch the very breath of his touch.
And the exquisitely beautiful, fragile sounds that
came from his fingers ! The unfathomable harmonies, the capricious design, the deep mystic
significance of his creations. All the progressive
musical world—professional press and uninitiated
laity—revelled in these none too frequent festal
nights.

The last concert of the season 1914-15 was
to take place in Moscow on April 11, 1915. But
fate decided otherwise. On April 4 Scriabin
returned from Petrograd where he had just played.
Feeling unwell he took to his bed on April 7. A
furuncle developed on his upper lip, on the same
spot as once previously. The fever was rising
rapidly. The best physicians of Moscow were
summoned to his bedside, there ensued consultation after consultation, but all was in vain. The
infection spread to the whole face. Scriabin
suffered pitifully. There was still some hope on

April 10, but when pleurisy set in all was over. He died at 8 a.m. on April 14. The noble and lofty mind, the titanic genius, the daring conqueror was snatched away from this earth on the eve of new revelations.

PART II

CHAPTER VII

Ties and Bonds

IN spite of his revolutionary course Scriabin is as much a child of the Russian school of music as any of his more conservative contemporaries—Glazunov, Rachmaninov, Medtner. He grew up in a musical environment replete with certain traits that belonged to Russia, and to Russia only, and they left their strong mark on him, clinging to him throughout his evolution and unendangered by it.

By the year 1892, the year of Scriabin's entry into the wide world, the Russian school had its established traditions. The Moscow and St. Petersburg conservatoires of music were now a quarter of a century old and had ground out methods of training young composers that in thoroughness were not one inch behind those of the big Italian training centres of the sixteenth century. In St. Petersburg the magnetic revolutionary influence of the grand amateurs—the " mighty band "—had given way to the Beliaev circle, composed for the most part of highly equipped and academically minded musicians

with conservative tendencies. Rimski-Korsakov
in his "Chronicle of my musical life" (p. 249)
gives the following summary of the distinctive
features of the above two phases in Russian
music :

"The Balakirev circle (the 'mighty band')
coincided with the period of storm and stress in
the development of Russian music, the Beliaev
circle with the period of a steady march onward.
The Balakirev circle was revolutionary, the
Beliaev circle—progressive. The Balakirev circle
consisted of five members, not counting Lody-
shenski, who never accomplished anything, and
Liadov, who appeared later : Balakirev, Cui,
Moussorgski, Borodin, and myself (the French
have up to this day preserved for us the appella-
tion 'les cinq'). The Beliaev circle was
numerous and grew as time went on. All the
five members of the former were subsequently
acknowledged as important representatives of
Russian musical art ; the latter was varied in its
composition : it contained important composers
as well as lesser lights and even non-creative
artists, conductors, such as Dutsch, or executant
soloists, such as N. S. Lavrov. The Balakirev
circle consisted of technically weak musicians,
almost amateurs, who fought their way by sheer
force of creative genius, force that sometimes

stood in the place of technique, and sometimes, as often with Moussorgski, was insufficient in itself to fill out the gaps. The Beliaev circle, on the other hand, consisted of composers and musicians, who were in full possession of technical training. The Balakirev circle considered Beethoven the first musician of •interest to them ; the Beliaev circle revered not only its musical parents, but also grandparents and forefathers, as far back as Palestrina. The Balakirev circle focused its attention on the orchestra, piano, chorus and vocal solos with orchestra, ignoring chamber music, vocal ensemble, chorus a capella, and string solos ; the Beliaev circle had in this respect much broader ideas. The Balakirev circle was highly intolerant, the Beliaev—more indulgent and eclectic. The Balakirev circle did not wish to learn, but made headway relying on its powers. It was successful and profited by its success. The Beliaev circle studied, attaching a great importance to technical perfection ; it also made headway but more slowly and more securely. The Balakirev circle hated Wagner and pretended not to notice him ; the Beliaev circle scrutinized Wagner with great care and respect. The relations of the former circle to its head resembled those of the pupil to the master and older brother ; such relations became fainter as each of the younger brothers

was growing mature, of which fact a great deal
has been said repeatedly ; Beliaev on the other
hand was not the head of his circle, but its
centre. . . ."

All these points of distinction were clearly
manifested in Rimski-Korsakov himself, once the
messmate of Borodin's and Moussorgski's musical
orgies, and now the soul and leader of the
Beliaevists.   It was under his surveillance that
the new generation was growing up—staid, pains-
taking and original, but hardly overwhelming.
It was into this circle that Scriabin was welcomed
at the outset of his musical career.   And, to be
sure, there were many common bonds.   There
was Liadov, a meticulous miniature writer,
enamoured of Chopin and Schumann and imitat-
ing them closely in his piano works ; there was
Glazunov, a born contrapuntist, weaving mas-
sively the texture of his symphonies, a musician
of unshaken solidity and logic ; there was Felix
Blumenfeld, a writer of preludes with many an
appassionato climax, and sometimes a genuine
note of pathos and trembling ; there were many
others more or less akin to the above.   Do we
not find certain strings in Scriabin's nature that
responded to the overscrupulousness of Liadov,
to the stern logic of Glazunov, and to the
"accumulations" of Blumenfeld ? Indeed we do,

and even the most violent harmonic convulsions of his later years could not efface them. And up to a certain point the Beliaevists acclaimed Scriabin as a better and stronger exponent of the creed that was so dear to them. But gradually his harmonic idiom became too baffling for them to comprehend. Liadov was the first to break his allegiance ; he carried it hardly beyond Scriabin's youthful, Chopinesque period. Glazunov and Rimski-Korsakov retreated after the Divine Poem and showed little understanding for the Poem of Ecstasy. Blumenfeld remained a pioneer of Scriabin's works longer than any of his associates, frequently produced the Poem of Ecstasy, but even he did not venture into the regions of " Prometheus."

Scriabin's ties with Moscow were still stronger. In his native city the influence of the mighty band had never been felt. The first big figure on the Moscow musical horizon, Tchaikovski, showed marked hostility towards any obtrusive manifestation of nationalism, and gloried in his admiration for the classics, Mozart in particular. Then came a man who once for all established the traditions for the Moscow conservatoire. This was Taneiev. He fully justified the title of the " Russian Netherlander " bestowed on him since his death in 1915: for his archaic austereness reached back to the days of the great Josquin. In

F

his illuminating course on counterpoint in the conservatoire, as also in his own polyphonic closely wrought chamber music and orchestral works, he was furnishing a background to musical art in Russia, such as no other composer could have furnished single-handed. He was a grand imposing figure, and eminently influential in shaping Moscow's musical mentality. The works of the younger Moscow generation— Glière, Rachmaninov, Medtner, for the most part direct pupils of Taneiev—are characterized by perfect structural design, a severe logic in harmonies and modulations, and if not a strictly polyphonic yet a thickset method of writing achieved mainly by an elaborate handling of the inner parts. In these its characteristics Moscow was a very stronghold against all impressionist tendencies, and it is herein that lies Scriabin's undoubted descent from the Russian school. Are not all the above traits minutely reproduced down to his last works, in strange contrast to the nature itself of his harmonies? It was this that saved him from diffuseness on his new harmonic path and made his daring innovations comprehensible to the more susceptible of his contemporaries.

So continuous is the development of Scriabin's musical personality that it is only with the greatest difficulty that one is able to draw lines of demarca-

tion between the different phases of his creative
activity. By imperceptible degrees he leads us
out of the domains of tonality into those of his
upper partial tone harmonies.* In studying his
works opus by opus it is well-nigh impossible to
tell at what particular juncture one has passed the
boundaries of definite key relationship ; and finding oneself in the " beyond " regions one is hardly
perplexed : the revolution has come about by such
gentle evolutionary means. Scriabin himself
could not have been conscious of any break or
cleavage in his output : he thought of all his
works, from beginning to end, as hewn out of the
same material. Witness his concert programmes
where the early harmonically simple works appear
side by side with the latest and most complex.
But if from a musical point of view a grouping
by periods is impracticable, there have been
psychologically in Scriabin's course two clear and
distinct sections. The first and shorter one is
the influence of Chopin. Under the ægis of
Chopin all his early works up to the 1st symphony
(op. 26) were composed. But about the time of
the latter work (1900) a new creative impulse

---

* Scriabin's last works, such as *e.g.* the Prelude op. 74, N1,
show an unmistakable approach to ultrachromaticism. Whether or
no he would have ultimately resorted to tertia-tones or quarter-
tones remains an open question. We must, however, bear in mind
his irresistible gravitation towards the piano, a tempered instrument
which claims ninety per cent. of his entire output.

completely supplanted the influence of the Polish
master. This was the Mystery idea, at first
vague, intangible, then assuming more and more
definite forms. It kept flickering before Scriabin's
mind, inciting him to grand achievement, but
whenever he felt that he had at last clutched it,
ready to embody it in an unheard-of synthesis
of arts, it invariably evanesced. Like a *fata
Morgana* it lured the gigantic mind of the musician
to supreme efforts, but every time he thought he
had entered the sanctuary, the image was glimmer-
ing as before in the distance. On his path in
quest of it, Scriabin's spirit traversed many a
fanciful kingdom : that of sensual pleasure and
satanic allurement (1901–1905),* of languor,
ecstasy, and divine creation (1905–1909), of
nature's wonders, thunder, lightning and cataracts
(1909–1912), and finally some magic, radiant, and
peaceful kingdom (1912–1914), from which there
seemed but one step to the Mystery, the step that
was frustrated by death. And while he was pour-
ing forth work after work—in magnitude com-
parable only to the loftiest there is in music—he
kept talking and thinking of the Mystery. However, this latter was something that mankind in
its present state was not prepared to embrace.
Scriabin was not blind to this fact. So one year
before the end, abandoning everything else, he

* It is here that Scriabin encounters Liszt.

determined to precipitate the advent of the Mystery, and in his daring brain conceived the so-called " Initial Act " to the Mystery, a sort of rehearsal that was to prepare mankind for the ultimate mysterious rite and worship.

CHAPTER VIII

A Soaring Elf

THE earliest period of Scriabin's creative
activity bears the imprint of an exceeding light-heartedness, a soaring disposition, now playful, now slightly melancholy, always
exquisite, poetic, and caressing. There is as yet
no deeper desire in this music than to meander
gracefully in the regions of the utmost refinement
and occasionally strike a note presentient of
coming perturbations. Here all is still and cloudless, and Scriabin revels in the ease and spontaneity
with which everything has come to him; but he
has not yet traversed the hypnotic influence of
another master-mind and circles to and fro in an
enchanted sphere.

Scriabin was not the first Russian musician to
fall under the sway of Chopin. The music of
the romantics had struck deep root in Russia:
Balakirev and his disciples of the mighty band
discarded classicism in favour of the romantic
spirit, as foreshadowed in Beethoven's last period
and appearing with full force in Schumann, Berlioz,
and Liszt. Chopin was as a model coupled with

the above mainly by the instrumentality of César Cui. A Frenchman by descent and a pupil of the Polish composer Moniuszko, Cui was just the right person to become Chopin's apologist in Russia, and in his own piano works established a style of Chopinesque music with flashes of Schumann-like humour and rhythm that came to be firmly embedded in Russia. It has reappeared later in Liadov, Arenski and many others of minor importance. But in no one was there a closer assonance of spirit with Chopin than in the young Scriabin. The exquisite handling of the piano—from early childhood Scriabin's favourite instrument—the power of inspired improvisation, a rare aristocracy of taste and an element of salon-like gracefulness : all these traits rendered him closely akin to the Polish master. Scriabin's early works (op. 1–25) accordingly breathe a Chopinesque atmosphere. But Scriabin is far from being a mere imitator. He is Chopin's rightful successor, and, as such, carries to an extreme certain peculiarities of Chopin's style. What lay in the background with Chopin comes to the fore in Scriabin : the music grows in nervousness (observe Scriabin's famous rubato playing and the innumerable indications to this effect in the preludes and sonatas) ; the tissue becomes closer and more compact, the writing neater and more scrupulous than even Chopin's. The number of dissonances increases as a result of an almost boundless use of suspensions : hardly has one little knot been untied in one of the parts when one or two more crop up in another. This, however, only enhances Scriabin's formal purity and the exceeding polish of his style.

Scriabin's first works appeared in print in the Jurgenson edition in 1893 and passed more or less unnoticed. Though they are full of melodic charm and ingenuity, and show signs of unusual harmonic progressions, their Chopinesque background made it difficult for them to attract attention at that time as something striking and out of the way. In the next few years Scriabin conquered the sympathies of the Beliaev circle and began to publish his works in the Beliaev edition. These include the first sonata (F minor, op. 6), a powerful work for a youth, conceived on a large scale, and containing many an anticipation of later ideas. But it is not till we come to the year 1897 that we are confronted by the overwhelmingly conspicuous personality of the young musician. This year brought no less than forty-seven short preludes written at various times and collected in five sets (op. 11, 13, 15, 16, 17). Here we can at once discern points of departure from Chopin and at the same time nail down certain traits of the real Scriabin : on the one hand a marvellous structural symmetry of the whole, obtained chiefly through the invariable presence of the simple clear-cut 4-bar phrase (see op. 11, N23, op. 16, N5), and also through a somewhat stereotyped modulating plan in which the chromatic sequence is a noted feature (see op. 11, N7, op. 15, N5) ; on the other hand an extraordinary richness of each separate bar, consisting of hardly two identical beats and exhibiting the most fanciful delineation and the most dazzling contours (see op. 11, N5, op. 16, N3). Other peculiarities are occasional complex ratios between the notes of the right and left hands (5 : 4, 6 : 5, 6 : 4, etc.), overlapping accompaniment figures, the abundance of suspensions mentioned above (op. 17, N6 is an extreme instance), and an unusual wealth of rubato time (see op. 17, N3). But above all it is the prevalence of soaring, ecstatic moods that unveils the true Scriabin from his Chopinesque coverlet (see op. 16, N2, op. 11, NN1, 10, 19). In magnificent contrast to the above are those preludes in which a lovely pastoral resignation reigns supreme (see op. 11, N15, op. 13, N3, op. 15, N1).

These antagonistic sides of the young Scriabin's temperament are wonderfully blended in the capital work that appeared in the following year, 1898—the second sonata op. 19. The first of its two movements—an Andante—is perhaps the most gorgeously fanciful and capricious of all

Scriabin's early works. Harmonically it is simpler than a good deal of Scriabin's contemporary music, and it does not abound in modulations, as its sister sonata N3, op. 23 ; on the contrary it shows a tendency to linger in one key. But its melodic elaboration is stupendous : one little melodic wave chases another in poetic playfulness, the accompaniment, thickly woven on broad lines, is all nerve and refinement. The second movement is an impetuous Presto, an onslaught of unabating fierceness. The sonata, as a whole, reveals to us the quintessence of the youthful composer, his superb individuality at an early stage of his development, his power of absorbing all extraneous influences—even that of Chopin is not prominent here.

Upon the heels of this sonata followed the third in F sharp minor (op. 23). This monumental work—alone of all Scriabin's sonatas it has four movements—shows us the composer at the cross-roads. One road pointed towards working out his melodies polyphonically—the result being a compact horizontal tissue, a massive whole in the manner of Bach and Taneiev. The other road beckoned towards the refining of the harmonic units producing a vertical line of the utmost complexity, while retaining the clear-cut, loosely jointed and symmetrical periods. There was but one choice for Scriabin : the strictest articulateness of musical speech was a prime necessity to him. So he clung with a passionate devotion to the childlike simplicity of his general contours and gave free vent to his reformatory tendencies in the medium of harmony. Such were the conflicting traits of his musical personality: a daring innovator of the twentieth century he is in the matter of structure not more complicated than Mozart.

Crystal clear in its orderly 4-bar periods, masterly united in its four movements, wonderfully pianistic and sonorous—the third sonata is also an unmistakable proof of Scriabin's descent from the Russian school. Witness the severeness and rigidity of the modulations in the finale : we can almost see in them Medtner's stern look. In this same concluding movement Scriabin uses for the first time a device that became habitual with him all through his next period : at the end of the work he brings, in a terrific jubilant climax, the main andante or lento theme—see fourth sonata, Poème Divin, fifth sonata. In the third sonata Scriabin saw his last touching-point with Chopin, though a parting tribute was paid to the Polish master in the 9 mazurkas of op. 25.

At this juncture of his course the Mystery idea dawned on Scriabin and gradually stamped out *all* influences. That of Chopin, however, from now on belongs to bygone days.

CHAPTER IX

The Elf v. The Titan

"THE spirit (the creative principle) is conscious of a polarity of the masculine and feminine elements, the one active, the other passive, the will and the resistance. The latter element, inactive and inert, becomes crystallized in the immobility of the material forms, in the World with its manifold phenomena. The separated poles reach in their separation a culminating point : the complete materialization and differentiation, the loss of any connection with the Deity. (In art—a division of its branches, formerly united, and the development of each branch in itself.) At this extreme point there arises a reaction in favour of a reunion : the World's love for the Spirit and vice versa—a mystical Eros. The purpose of the separation is achieved : the creative substance has left its mark on the matter and there begins a process of dematerialization, reunion. (In art— the union of separate arts, their synthesis.) This reunion is completed by means of the *Mystery*— the mystical act of the caresses of the Spirit and the World. There will ensue a mystical union taking a form that cannot as yet be comprehended. This will be universal Death and new Life, a world cataclysm destroying physical life. . . ." Thus Leonid Sabaneiev, one of Scriabin's closest philosophical coadjutors in the years of maturity. According to Scriabin and Sabaneiev the Mystery was to be the concluding act of the life of our race, a final manifestation of its vitality, a colossal mystical cataclysm separating our perishing race from a new-born race (attention was drawn to a similar extinction of races previous to ours). All the finest creative powers of our race, heretofore dismembered in the different branches of art, would be united in the Mystery.

Some future critic of philosophy will doubtlessly assign to this cosmic idea its due place and importance in the history of thought, discourse on Scriabin's originality or indebtedness to other philosophic systems. Our concern is to show its relation to Scriabin's music, and in this respect it looms paramount as an undying source of the most divine inspiration to the composer. All that was best in his creative mind and soul Scriabin allotted to the Mystery. But while in the process of creating his music the horizon of his vision and ideas widened and widened, what he intended to be embodied in the Mystery satisfied him no longer, and he utilized this old material for other musical works. This was the way in which grew up all his larger and most of his smaller works beginning with the 1st symphony. In a certain sense they are all offshoots from the Mystery.

The above conception of the Mystery was not instantaneous with Scriabin. It was the result of long years of mental intensification. Its germ can be traced to the diary of the youthful composer wherein we find the words : " I am transported with gladness that is in me. If the world could only partake of an atom of the joy that is mine, the world would suffocate in bliss." About the time of the fading away of the influence of Chopin (1899) Scriabin thought of "a grand festival of humanity " that would unite all arts. His adoration of art in all its manifestations was most exuberant. Curiously, however, there had never been a time when he was content with the formula of art for art's sake. Religion and art were always closely connected in his mind and a strange magic power was ascribed to them. At this stage his mystical ideas found their musical embodiment in the 1st symphony op. 26.

It was significant that from the moment new startling thoughts had effaced Chopin's haunting shadow, Scriabin for the first time took to the orchestra as a means of expressing himself (the little " Reverie " op. 24 was composed about the same time). He was, however, then only partly successful. The orchestra was a new field to him, and he accordingly proceeded but cautiously. There is less boldness in his harmonies: there is no such soaring imagination as in the second and third sonatas. It seems as though Scriabin was afraid to break away from the academic style in these first orchestral attempts of his. A well-meaning docility permeates the 1st symphony, as also the " Reverie," which is a little out of keeping with Scriabin's musical personality. In spite of this there is charm enough in the first five movements of the symphony (the latter consists of the usual four movements framed into a sort of prelude and "postlude"), the vivacious little Scherzo is a perfect gem of construction, the harmonies of the middle Lento are interesting and try to keep pace with Scriabin's contemporary piano pieces. But in the final movement, the "postlude," just where he was giving vent to his newly formulated ideas, Scriabin lamentably missed fire : an academic and conventional fugue is ill-suited for a hymn of praise to art. And it was for no less a purpose that Scriabin here added chorus and soloists to the orchestra. Scriabin himself must have felt the inadequacy of this finale, for soon after the completion of the symphony he spoke with fervour of writing an opera with the superartist for its hero. But no opera was ever written and the reason is clear. The essence of

Scriabin's mental process was to bring about and take part in the mystical and religious rite itself. A mere representation of it, such as an opera could provide, was of no interest to him. So the hero of the opera became Scriabin himself, and the opera merged into the Mystery. So it happened that Scriabin's own creative personality found itself in the centre of his cosmic conception. He imagined himself endlessly creating, overcoming self-imposed obstacles, eternally striving with no achievement in view, just for the sake of divine play (Jeu Divin).

The Mystery was acquiring a definite place in his cosmogony : the Spirit of the Universe was making manifestations of the Universal Symphony to suffering humanity through spiritual centres among men—his Messiahs. One of these Messiahs Scriabin imagined himself to be ; a belief that with years became as firm as a rock, and the potent source of the terrific strength and vitality of his inspiration. And while absorbed in this process of thought, Scriabin's musical development was taking its relentless course. Having initiated himself into the mysteries of orchestral writing, Scriabin struck out a bolder note in the 2nd symphony op. 29 which followed hard upon the 1st. This symphony stands on the threshold of a new harmonic world which Scriabin made his own in his so-called transition period (1901–1905).

The main Allegro and the middle Andante are in this respect closely akin to the contemporaneous pianoforte works op. 30–42. In the other movements, especially the Tempestuoso and the pompous finale, Scriabin still feels ill at ease and speaks quite unconvincingly.

In all these early orchestral works of Scriabin there is clearly noticeable an outward inclination in the direction of Wagner. The 2nd symphony, in particular, is rather heavily scored, and the blazing diatonic fanfares of its finale betray the author of " Tannhäuser." But Wagner's influence on Scriabin was ephemeral and lay wholly on the surface : the passages in Scriabin nearest to him, like the above finale, were invariably the least successful. Besides the formlessness and melodic continuity of the author of " Tristan," which must have been a perfect nightmare to our puristic composer, there was fundamentally a deep-rooted and insurmountable difference between the two great reformers : Wagner's music, though appearing complicated when taken as a whole (in its biggest formal units), was simple and easy when split up into bars and beats—the smallest units. Exactly the opposite prevailed in Scriabin : his musical thinking led him " to construct clear symmetrical edifices out of the most precious and refined material."

There was, however, another great musician

G

whose moods, though not affecting in the slightest Scriabin's purely musical and harmonic development, were yet to a certain extent reproduced in the general atmosphere of the works of the coming transition period.   This was Liszt.

CHAPTER X

A Streak of Diabolism

DIABOLIC moods were not foreign to Scriabin at more than one juncture of his path towards the Mystery. We encounter them for the first time in the period of transition that confronts us in the years after the 1st symphony. Scriabin's joyous adoration of art was taking the form of a high spiritual exaltation, an infatuation for beauty, and a deification of the creative impulse. The creative artist was becoming the ruler of the Universe. Yet his god-like features were sometimes queerly transformed into a satanic grimace : he seemed to be God or Satan at will.

Such moods as these thrust Scriabin into a curious contact with Liszt, who was subject to a similar capacity for complete transformation. In this contact we find an absolutely subconscious reaction on Scriabin of the great Weimar Musician, otherwise so far removed from him, not only in time, surroundings, development, but also in general mentality. There was nothing of that assonance of spirit between the mature Scriabin and Liszt that is so prominent in the young

Scriabin and Chopin. Liszt's musical personality lay, for the most part, completely outside the range of the forces that were shaping the maturing mind of Scriabin. But in the chameleonic Liszt there was the somewhat satanic quality of " sincere affectation." It appears with great frankness in Liszt's B-minor sonata and in the Mephisto Waltz, and it reappears in Scriabin's Fantasia op. 28, the Tragic Poem op. 34, and particularly in the Satanic Poem op. 36—note the epithets: amorosissimo, riso, ironico. A demoniac, corrupt humour challenges here the loftiness of Scriabin's aim trying to lure the composer into baser regions. Triumphantly overcome in the Divine Poem these devilish fits continued to pester Scriabin even at a much later stage—see " Etrangeté " op. 63, and the poisonous 9th sonata op. 68.

But while only a few of the works of this period are tinged with diabolism, all of them reveal a sublime spiritual exaltation. It is primarily in this sense that there is a close common bond uniting the 4th sonata op. 30 and all the manifold preludes and poems that were poured forth for the most part in the year 1903 (up to op. 39).* Another strong bond exists here in the form of

---

* It is interesting to observe that the years of Scriabin's professorship in Moscow (1898–1903) were not all too productive. It was the moment he had resigned casting off all fetters that the above piano works were produced in a fit of inspiration—Summer 1903 to February 1904.

a new harmonic outlook which Scriabin has meanwhile adopted. The passing dissonances in which his earlier works abounded now cede before fundamental dissonances. The background to these is supplied by a new chord : the chord of the ninth with the simultaneously augmented and diminished fifth—C E F sharp A flat D. Augmented chords (especially the French sixth) are scattered with great profuseness, major and minor triads become rarer and rarer, appearing still at the end of the composition and of very elaborate cadences, but hardly ever at the start (see 4th sonata, Satanic Poem, Poems op. 32, prelude op. 27, N1). This shift of harmonic thought has already affected the main Allegro of the 2nd symphony op. 29, but in the other movements Scriabin still clings to a more or less accepted idiom. However, thanks to this fine main Allegro, as also to the ravishingly beautiful Andante—there are again faint echoes of Liszt in the erotic music of this movement—this symphony must be regarded as an enormous advance on the somewhat conservative 1st symphony.

Beginning with the 4th sonata op. 30, a magnificently new harmonic kingdom is invaded. This work contains no trace of earlier influences. In its daring flight it soars high into radiant regions. Like the 3rd sonata, the theme of the introductory slow movement is worked up in a colossal climax at the end.　In point of construction this sonata is well on the way towards the one-movement sonatas that are to follow : its two movements are inseparable.　Henceforth there is no further instance in Scriabin's bigger works of a division into independent movements (the three phases of the Divine Poem are played uninterruptedly).　Possessed of beautifully curved, languid melodies, profusely savoured with luxurious chord-of-the-ninth harmonies, swayed by a wonderful rhythm—quietly uneven with groups of 3 against groups of 4 in the slow movement, and in the Prestissimo volando leaping in triplets the third note of which is a soaring rest—closely wrought with amazing stretches in the left hand, this sonata takes away one's breath, and when the sun shines forth in glorious light in the Coda (focosamente, giobilosco), we are left dumbfounded as after the occurrence of a natural phenomenon.

The fragrant and delicate Poem op. 32 N1 takes harmonically another step forward : at the beginning of its 2nd and 7th bars—not counting the up-beat—we find the future synthetic chord of " Prometheus" (see p. 99) in its entirety.　Only here it is still resolved through the chord of the ninth into the major triad.　This same poem in its crystal clear texture gives an ideal example of Scriabin's masterful part-writing and lovely incidental counterpoint.　The Promethean harmony reappears in preludes N2 and N3 of op. 37. The last prelude of this set (op. 37) with its obscured tonality is a sort of preparation for Scriabin's new harmonic system. Op. 31 N1 is similarly obscured and modulates strikingly from D flat to G and from G flat to C in two symmetrical sections. Still more daring yet strictly logical modulations are revealed in the fantastic and melodious arabesque op. 39 N1, and the cadence of op. 39 N3 shows such exquisite artistic feeling as to baffle all comprehension. Ranging from purely experimental fragments, like op. 31 N4, op. 33 N3, op. 39 N4, to the most powerful emotional documents, like the poem op. 32 N2, or the preludes op. 37 N1, 2, op. 35 N2, and op. 39 N1, 3, the piano works of this period are a noble and memorable page in the history of Scriabin's evolution.

Before his departure to Switzerland Scriabin often spoke of some union of all mankind, of some grand festival wherein the orchestra would play a prominent part. As a suitable place for this festival he then designated Switzerland. Soon afterwards he departed thither in order to accomplish the writing of music, " such as had never been heard before." This was to be the Divine Poem, op. 43 (also called the 3rd symphony). It is only a further step towards the Mystery, of which Scriabin now for the first time began to talk

in definite terms. The mere deification of the
creative impulse, which is characteristic of the
preceding piano works, no longer satisfied him.
He now began to identify such impulse with the
divine play of the free powers of self-asserting
individuality. His Spirit was thus passing from
struggle through enjoyment to divine play. This
is the basis of the Divine Poem. Scriabin's wife
—Tatiana Feodorovna—has compiled the following programme to this monumental work, and it
was published with Scriabin's approval :

"The first movement of the Divine Poem
'Luttes' is the struggle between Man enslaved by
a personal God and the free Man, God in himself.
The latter is victorious, but when it comes to
proclaiming his divinity he finds that his will is too
weak for such a feat. He accordingly plunges
into the delights of the sensual world. This is the
second movement 'Voluptés.' Then from the
bottom of his being there rises in him a sublime
power that helps him to overcome his weakness,
and in the last movement 'Jeu Divin' the liberated
spirit gives himself up to the joy of a free
existence."

Beginning and ending with a proud challenge,
the gallant music of the first movement flows along,
now bursting into a joyous major, now clouded
by tempestuous passages, always full of human
tragedy. In the second part we are carried off

into another world couched in rapturous harmonies, a world of sensual delights, suave and caressing. Then comes the radiant finale with an enormous climax on the theme of the slow movement (compare the 3rd and 4th sonatas). Here for the first time Scriabin has found a suitable orchestral language to express his grand visions. Harmonically the Divine Poem is a typical product of the transitional period : it still clings to the older traditions ; yet it is evident that having reached this point of harmonic evolution the composer cannot fail to progress still further, and will soon oust the remaining major and minor triads. In one respect, however, this symphony is less advanced than the contemporaneous piano pieces : it is built throughout on broad, sustained melodies, while the tendency with Scriabin, as he develops, is to replace such melodies by short, characteristic themes —see the Poem of Ecstasy—until finally melody with him loses its independence from harmony.

Taken as a whole, the Divine Poem is a work of art of the most daring conception. Its idiom, while it contains here and there faint reminiscences of Liszt and even of " Tristan," is nevertheless so bewilderingly original as to constitute an epoch in itself. At the cross-roads of his evolution Scriabin has here erected an imposing monument of everlasting beauty. And now we can observe his final departure into radiant regions.

CHAPTER XI

The Wonderland of Ecstasy

SCRIABIN'S philosophic system was in the main his own. But there is no denying the fact that it was strengthened from various other sources. Scriabin had a peculiar capacity for picking out, after a casual acquaintance with some philosophy, certain aspects of it which tended to clarify his own thoughts. He never penetrated deeply into any system : he was too sure of the inevitableness of his own. So it was when in the preceding years in Moscow he met Prince S. N. Troubetskoi, a pupil of the great Vladimir Soloviov. He liked the Prince, but there is no indication of his ever having studied Soloviov seriously. Yet there is undoubtedly a certain affinity in the Mystery idea to the teaching of Soloviov. After the completion of the Divine Poem he was thrust into contact with theosophy. This was a more lasting spell. He kept up from that time (1905) a constant intercourse with the leaders of theosophic thought. He even adopted for a while the theosophic definitions, but very soon substituted for them

his own and the more primeval Upanishad term-
inology.   The theosophers were also responsible
for the fact that Scriabin's looks turned towards
India.   It was this mysterious country that now
became the object of his secret aspirations, and
very soon it assumed its place in the Mystery plan,
ousting Switzerland for good and all.   He read
omnivorously all the available literature on India
and experienced a keen delight in finding what a
close resemblance there was between his cosmos
and the mysteries of the East.   His thoughts
expanded, became more crystallized.   He acquired
a haunting feeling of being on the eve of the
realization of the Mystery, and thrust into an
astounded world offshoots from it in the form of
the Poem of Ecstasy op. 54, the 5th sonata
op. 53, and smaller works for the piano.   These
works are characterized by a further radical shift
of harmonic ideas.

Up to the 5th sonata Scriabin still regards the
chord of the ninth with all its modifications and
inversions as an essentially dominant harmony
which is ultimately resolved into the tonic.   In
the 5th sonata (also in the "Trois Morceaux"
op. 52) the chord C E G B flat D ceases to demand
a resolution and becomes a sort of independent
five-note consonance with its root on C.   This
consonance definitely ejects the old triad.   Thus
the beginning of the Languido in the 5th sonata

would under the older system be a sort of dominant harmony in B major. Scriabin, however,
puts six sharps which shows that he thinks of it
as belonging to the key of F sharp major. It is
as if Scriabin rejoiced at having cut himself loose
from the compulsion to resolve the chord of the
ninth : the 5th sonata and the other works of
this period (see " Fragilité " and " Poème ailé "
op. 51) abound in this chord as also in the chords
of the 11th and 13th in their pure form (the
French sixth disappears entirely). This fact
brings about a curious contact of Scriabin with
Debussy and " Pelleas "—" the realm of the chord
of the ninth ": in a few scattered places the
shadow of the great Frenchman seems to arise
only in order to dwindle away at once before
Scriabin's towering logic and consistency. However, the Promethean chord, which had cropped up
in isolated spots in the preceding period, also
makes itself felt more and more, and begins to
form the foundation of whole episodes (see the
Meno Vivo on p. 12 of the sonata).

In point of construction the 5th sonata finally
embraces the one-movement form. In adopting
this form for his sonatas Scriabin, however, did
not completely discard the other movements. He
found room for them within the frame of the one
movement. The different parts of the sonata—
the slow movement, the scherzo, the finale—all

become episodes of one part. Thus in the first introduction to the 5th sonata we can discern a sort of scherzo, in the second introduction—a sort of Andante or Adagio. Both these episodes recur at various junctures of the movement. In the unusually extended codas of the later sonatas we can observe the embodiment of a kind of finale. Thus we find in Scriabin, as he progresses, a concentration of creative activity : the primary elements of sonata structure are abandoned and all stress is laid on the secondary elements—the structure of periods, phrases, and harmonic progressions ; an articulateness and dismemberment of musical speech that is without parallel in modern music.

The 5th sonata has been likened to a piece of wizardry, a deed of black magic, illumined by the rays of a black sun (see Eugene Gunst's book on Scriabin). Its impetuosity alternating with a caressing languor, the legerdemain of the Prestos in their radiant mixture of B major and F sharp major, and the wild orgiastic rhythm of the Allegros, combine to produce an uncanny impression. The other piano pieces of this period equally reflect the celestial spheres in which Scriabin's mind was labouring. Most of them are designated now by descriptive titles and collected in five sets (op. 49, 51, 52, 56, 57) ranging between the years 1906 and 1908. Harmonically they are closely akin to the 5th sonata, and in their alternation of ecstatic, fragile, and languid moods surround by a brilliant halo the capital work of this period : the Poem of Ecstasy.*

Scriabin's Ecstasy is the joy of unrestrained activity. The Universe (the Spirit) is an eternal creation with no outward aim or motive—a divine play with worlds. However, the creating Spirit —the Universe at play—does not himself realize the absolute value of creation ; he has subjected himself to a purpose, has made his activity a means towards another end. But the quicker the pulse of life beats in him, the more rapid becomes its rhythm, the clearer it dawns on him that he is through and through creation alone— an end in itself—that life is play. And when the Spirit, having reached the climax of his activity, which is gradually tearing him away from the delusion of utility and relativity, will comprehend his substance—an unrestrained activity—then Ecstasy will arise. The Poem of Ecstasy is thus a sort of cosmogony. The autobiographic element in Scriabin's bigger works, which was so prominent in the 2nd and 3rd symphonies, gives way before a cosmic conception of unheard-of dimensions, reincarnated in music as baffling as it is convincing. The amazing sonority of the

* See "Fragilité," "Poème ailé," and "Danse languide " op. 51, "Enigme" and "Poème languide " op. 52, "Ironies " and "Nuances " op. 56, and "Désir " and "Caresse dansee " op. 57.

work is attained alike through a masterful use
of the orchestra and a canonic and figurative
development of the themes.   Of the latter there
are no less than 8.   But there is hardly a trace
left in them of the broad cantilena of the Divine
Poem.   They are either short characteristic flour-
ishes like the will, the self-assertion, and the
menace themes, or gliding chromatic wails like the
theme of yearning which forms the opening
phrase of the Poem, and the 2 main themes of
the exposition.   The structure of the Poem is
crystal clear, and the correlation of such keys as
are left in Scriabin's harmonic scheme as naive as
in a Mozart sonata (C, G— in exposition, C, C—
in recapitulation)   The abundance of themes
disturbs the symmetrical plan of the Poem not at
all, for some of them form the connecting and
concluding parts of the exposition, while others
are brought in at the culminating point of the
working-out section.   Besides, their brevity and
intertwinement with the texture of the whole
work prevent their taking shape in the mind of
the listener as superimposed or unexploited
material.   The working out of the Poem is of a
coherence and sonoric beauty that are bewildering,
and at certain culminating points Scriabin plunges
into a dazzling orgy of sound.   Rolling trills
gradually take possession of the whole orchestra,
with rapid descending and ascending passages in

the higher register of the wind. In the Coda Scriabin brings the self-assertion theme in augmentation, a favourite device of his (see Divine Poem, 3rd and 4th sonatas). If, in addition, we remember that he is moving in an entirely new harmonic idiom, with only an occasional triad at the close of cadences, the imposing grandeur of the Poem and its epoch-making significance will become still more evident.

Yet in spite of the new world of sound revealed in the " Poem of Ecstasy " there are still invisible threads that tie it to the old world. For a scrupulously logical and consequent musician, such as Scriabin, it was but a gradual burning of boats. Only two years separate the Poem of Ecstasy from " Prometheus "—Scriabin's last orchestral utterance—but it is in those two fateful years (1908–1910) that the gulf between new and old became actually unbridgeable.

CHAPTER XII

SUCH is the startling motto of Balmont, the prince of Russian poets, whose poetry in its flight towards the sun of individualism is so closely akin to Scriabin's music ! Truly sunlight is this " ocean of molten, seething gold " * that is exposed to us in the Poem of Fire.

" Prometheus " is the creative principle, the active energy of the Universe. There is the same thread of cosmic evolution as in Scriabin's previous works. Beginning with the yearning phase the Spirit passes through a period of materialization back to its true aerial substance. Carried off in a wild orgiastic dance, it is finally united with God.

At the time of the composition of " Prometheus " (1909–1910) the Mystery flickered before Scriabin's mind with unprecedented strength, acquiring clearer and clearer contours. The vast universal importance of Scriabin's art, its close connection with religion and ritual, its

---

* An expression of V. G. Karatuigin.

97   H

elemental force and the striking forms into which
it shaped itself—all this came to a brilliant climax
in this Scriabin's last orchestral work. Certain
elements of the Mystery are obviously to be
found here. In addition to the orchestra (which
already in the Poem of Ecstasy had grown to
colossal proportions and included the organ),
" Prometheus " requires the piano and a chorus.
This chorus Scriabin wished to see dressed in
white robes so as to give the whole a festal,
ritualistic appearance. Is not this a foretaste of
the Mystery in which all to the number of 2000
were to be performers ? But most remarkable of
all : the score of " Prometheus " provides for a
clavier à lumière. This new instrument—shaped
and played like a toneless piano—would by means
of a huge reflector cast the concert hall into the
most gorgeous symphony of colours. Here is the
first practical step towards the unification of all
arts—one of the goals of the Mystery.*

The change from the " Ecstasy " to the
" Prometheus " harmonies comes out very clearly
in the two pieces of op. 59, composed immediately
preceding the Poem of Fire op. 60. The first
—a Poème—still abounds in the chord of the

* The faculty of combining sounds with colours Scriabin shared
with many a musician. The most notable example is Rimski-
Korsakov, who had an equivalent in colours for every tonality.
Scriabin's scheme does not in all points correspond with that of
Rimski-Korsakov, though fundamentally there is a good deal of
accord between them.

ninth, which is typical of the "Ecstasy" period. The second—a Prelude—is dominated throughout by the mystic Promethean chord. This magnificent chord is derived from some of the more dissonant upper partial tones of a sound (*e.g.* from the lower C the row of partial tones would be the following: C—c g c' e' g' b flat' c'' d'' e'' f sharp'' g'' a'' b flat'' b'' c' ''). The first ten partial tones came to their rights—as dissonances and consonances—before Scriabin. Thus Monteverde used the unprepared b flat of the above, Schumann and Chopin the unprepared d'', resolving them into what was considered a consonance. The Impressionists ceased to resolve these dissonances and herein encounter Scriabin in his "Poem of Ecstasy" period. Scriabin in his "Prometheus" and in isolated instances even before (see op. 32 and 37) opened up an unexploited region by receiving with one stroke the f sharp'' a'' and b flat'' (the 11th, 13th and 14th partial tones) into the family of *consonances*. He omitted the g'' (the 12th partial tone) owing to the retention in his harmonies of the diminished and augmented fifth (the f sharp and the a flat of the above). Having "discovered" his sounds, Scriabin proceeded to arrange them in ascending fourths: C F sharp B flat E A D. This chord is actually the only chord of "Prometheus," and upon analysis it will be found to embrace all the four kinds of triads (major, minor, diminished and augmented). That is why it has been called synthetic. The timbre of the synthetic harmony is clearest in the middle register, in the bass it becomes a low murmur, in the treble—a brilliant sheen.

Harmony in "Prometheus" finally assumes the function of melody : the latter, if divested of its harmonic basis, would undoubtedly lose most of its poignancy. Even the laconic themes of the Poem of Ecstasy seem long in comparison with the particles of themes that glitter in "Prometheus." But Scriabin goes still further. Not only does he seem to avoid a sustained theme, but sustained notes and sounds are equally abhorrent to him. He is afraid of their vulgarizing effect and makes use of continuous trills, little runs, appoggiaturas. This complete dematerialization and aerial quality become still more marked in the post-Promethean sonatas.

The structure of "Prometheus" is about as simple as that of the Poem of Ecstasy : an introduction, two main themes or their equivalents in Scriabin's new melodic language, a vastly complicated development section, wherein, however, the two above themes are kept in the background, a recapitulation of enormous grandeur, and finally a coda with a terrific climax at the end. There is no longer any trace of tonality : even the last F sharp major chord with every note of it trilled a whole tone upwards brings little satisfaction. Yet, in assuming the bass note of certain main chords to be its root, one can establish a strict proportion and symmetry between the 1st and 2nd themes, the exposition and the recapitulation, etc., etc. The cadences are highly marked, though less noticeable owing to the shift of the harmonies. As in his previous works Scriabin remains true to his formal purism. In the coda of " Prometheus " the usual device of enlarging the themes is for the first time inverted : from now on Scriabin preferred to bring them in diminution, in a kind of delirious dance (see 7th, 8th and 10th sonatas).

There is in " Prometheus " a union of the simple and complex, the highly refined and the highly overwhelming, that bespeak the most consummate and supreme artist in its creator. But not only do we find the everlasting struggle between Elf and Titan in this unheard-of work, but there is another struggle clearly evident from now on and unto the end : the Priest and Prophet have subdued the Artist into a position of subservience. " Prometheus " is the border line between art and religion, between the actual and the supernatural, a form of magic incantation. Incantational rhythms and convulsions, imperative hypnotic trumpet sounds, ecstatic emotionalism : all this tends to eliminate the Poem of Fire from the domain of pure art and place it in a category of its own. Scriabin—the mystagogue —has entered a sphere eminently congenial to him, and hurries along the inevitable path towards his cherished goal.

CHAPTER XIII

TOWARDS THE MYSTERY

IN rapid succession, during less than three years, Scriabin produced his last works for the piano. They include the five last sonatas, works of enormous significance, full of prophetic force, each of them a smaller Mystery. The instantaneousness with which all these works were conceived and affixed on paper, their compactness and consummate concentration, are little short of miraculous. A whole year before his cruel death, *i.e.* in 1914, he had said all he had to say prior to the crowning work of his life. Thenceforward there were no more offshoots, anticipations, side-tracks. He was bent on the colossal deed itself that challenged all the mighty resources of his genius.

In one point he had to concede to reality. The approximation of the Mystery itself, which was to be the end of the life of our race, was not within a human's power. So Scriabin had to content himself with the creation of the so-called "Initial Act," a sort of essaying of the Mystery, a mustering of the forces that were to take part

in the latter, a spiritual exercise of the vastest
dimensions.   Here Scriabin would combine the
parts of creator and high priest, always reserving
for himself the medium of music through which
to express himself most fitly.   For this treble rôle
he was training himself in his post-Promethean
works.

There is a new outburst of Satanism (see 7th,
9th sonatas, Masques and Etrangeté op. 63), but
after a period of despair and panic he resigns himself and embraces the azure fancy, caressing it in
the most radiant music ever imagined (see 8th,
10th sonatas, the Poems of op. 69).   Then there
comes a new passionate search : the priest is trying to cleanse himself by Fire (Vers la Flamme
op. 72, Guirlandes and Flammes sombres op. 73).
Scriabin has now definitely outgrown individualism.
His Ego has swallowed up the Universe.   In the
last five preludes op. 74 we are on the threshold
of the Mystery.   A pantheistic atmosphere pervades the music and we are witnessing a liturgic
act of surpassing majesty.

From a purely musical point of view every
one of the above creations is fraught with fresh
truth.   In the 6th and 7th sonatas Scriabin's
harmonies appear still more complex.   The
Promethean chord is further deformed by the
lowering of the 9th partial tone (the d″).   This
shifted semitone seems to enhance the troubled

element ("troublé") in the works of this period. While the 6th sonata is full of a new romanticism, passionate and stormy, we find in the 7th even elements of cruelty and harshness. This latter was Scriabin's favourite "white mass," a work full of trumpet calls and pealing, lightnings, cataracts, and icebergs. Its counterpart is the 9th sonata— the "black mass," a diabolic nightmare, a deed of black secret magic, the most perfidious piece of music ever conceived. In both these sonatas there is a marvellous contrast between the first and second themes, but, while in the 7th sonata the lovely second theme triumphs in the end over the powers of darkness, in the 9th the still more lovely second theme is poisoned and distorted by Evil incarnate. Scriabin was himself surprised at the creation of this truly satanic work and avoided playing it overmuch. He was enamoured of the 7th sonata, however, and played it with unparalleled, baffling skill and power. He was equally fond of the charming Poème-Nocturne op. 61 and the fickle and deceitful Masques and Etrangeté op. 63. These latter show how Scriabin's aristocratic refinement and salon-like grace remained intact in spite of his harmonic convulsions and the growing dimensions of his message to humanity.

The new stretch of violence over, we are face to face with further surprising entanglements. The 8th sonata with its new harmonic change—

the lowering of the 10th partial tone (the e″)—
brings us to the line where complexity and simplicity meet. Scriabin's harmonies seem to have
toppled over, and from now on appear much simpler
(see 8th sonata, Poem op. 69 N1, op. 71 N2, 10th
sonata). This is nothing but a delusion, however.
Psychologically and in relation to the whole context
they are still more complicated. Bright and
exuberant, the music of the 8th sonata speeds on,
a divine azure vault, the happiest and most care-
less of inspirations. Scriabin is loath to cut short
the heavenly length of this sonata ; again he
brings a vertiginous rhythm in the coda. Truly
a miracle, a phantom woven of delicate cobwebs,
a grandiose image reproduced in the most exquisite
manner. How different from its successor—the
9th sonata—where the fragrant main theme (here
the second), suffering gradual disfiguration, is
couched in the most hideous, grimacing harmonies,
and finally parades away in a grotesque march
movement. A veritable picture of Dorian Gray !

With the two poems of op. 69 Scriabin throws
open the doors into the radiant kingdom of the
10th and last sonata op. 70. Behold, still simpler,
crystalline harmonies, an almost transparent lucidity
of exposition, a powerful climax, and the now
indispensable whirlwind dance in the coda. And
then come the works of the year 1914—the lovely
poems of op. 71, the blazing red-hot " Vers la

Flamme," the beautifully contoured Guirlandes, the infernal Flammes sombres, and lastly the five preludes op. 74. These latter unfold in many respects a new page in Scriabin's writing. A partial change of method was already responsible for the apparent harmonic simplicity of the works beginning with the 8th sonata. Scriabin had up to then created new consonances vertically, preserving a stereotyped horizontal sequence : with the 8th sonata he inclines towards the reverse method —that of Wagner—and while his vertical harmonies seem simpler, their juxtaposition is much more complicated than in the works of the Promethean period. A further tendency to abandon his lifelong methods is noticeable in the preludes op. 74. There had never been any real counterpoint in Scriabin's writing, counterpoint in which harmony is the result of the intertwinement of the parts. With Scriabin harmony has always occupied a position of overwhelming pre-eminence. Thus his consonances and dissonances were fundamental, as with Beethoven or Chopin, and not passing, as with Bach, Schumann, or Taneiev. In his last work, however, we can observe symptoms of such passing harmonies, of a network of separate melodies. The 2nd and 4th preludes, in particular, offer a striking instance of chromatic passages turned to such contrapuntal account. NN 3 and 5 are simpler in character with their violent

figuration in the right hand, and absolutely unheard-of scales, marvellously expressive and full
of shrieking cruelty. N1 is a heart-rending cry.
On the whole, the prevailing mood in this last
work of Scriabin's is suffering, a mood by no
means common with him and a little disconcerting
on the eve of new revelations. The ominous
calm of the 2nd prelude—the most remarkable of
them all—is only a partial and rather dubious
compensation for the feeling of poignant grief
that pervades the others.

In the summer of 1914 Scriabin wrote down
the text to the "Initial Act" which he had
conceived about a year before. This text as well
as the first sketches of the music are carefully
preserved by the Scriabin society that was formed
soon after the master's decease. But the public
and critics are not yet in a position to judge its
nature. The war and the revolution have pre-
vented its publication, if such publication was at
all contemplated by Scriabin's executors. For the
text itself, though it evoked the enthusiastic
admiration of the poets Baltrushaitis and V.
Ivanov—two masters of form and poetic philosophy—would give only a poor conception of the
colossal creation that Scriabin had in mind.

One might well speculate as to the outcome of
it all : there were to be performers only, no listeners
or spectators. Their number was mentioned as

2000. Was it possible to find such a vast number
of people, not only initiated but also gifted with
executive talent ? All arts were to be represented
and blended in an unprecedented manner. There
was to be no simple counterpoint of musical parts,
or even elements of one and the same art, it
was to be a counterpoint of the various arts that
Scriabin's daring brain was concocting. Colours
were to be in counterpoint with sounds, words
with action or dancing. A melodic outline would
not remain " melodic," but might end by a plastic
movement, a stanza of poetry might merge into a
rainbow of colours to the background of the most
divine perfumes. And all this taking place in a
temple far away in India, in a temple of the semi-
globular shape reflected in water, so as to produce
the entire globe—the most perfect of all shapes.
Such baffling complexity has surely never been
born out of one single mind. Could one single
mind see it accomplished ? How to train a
following of the initiated ? Whom to entrust with
the singing and dancing ? Chaliapine and Karsa-
vina ? The performers would surely have to be
their equals in point of talent, yet also alive to the
mystic significance of the event.

It must be admitted that the technical
difficulties confronting Scriabin were enormous.
It would have taken years and years of quiet
preparation, of a step-by-step approximation of the

ultimate goal ; an undying enthusiasm and ardour
on the part of Scriabin himself and his friends.
Yet with all the obstacles confronting it, it was a
highly practical idea.   True, it would have been
wrecked by the turn of historic events, as we see
them now.   The war, which Scriabin   naively
hailed as the beginning of the world cataclysm,
and its fatal consequences, would have postponed
the realization of the " Initial Act " for at least a
generation, and it is doubtful if Scriabin would
have lived to take part in it.   But, assuming that
the pre-war culture had been allowed to thrive,
there was nothing insurmountable in the performance of the " Initial Act."

The Mystery itself could, of course, be nothing
but a far-distant dream, of which it was impossible
to speak in definite terms, and even Scriabin himself, intoxicated as he was by the idea, admitted
that the world was not yet prepared to accept it.
He believed, however, that shortly, perhaps in a
few years, a huge social wave would sweep across
humanity and, combining with the mystical wave,
would purge the world for the great cataclysm.

It was not given to the giant-musician to
realize the dream of his life : it was not given to
the world to enjoy peacefully the fruits of a high
spiritual culture.   The catastrophe of 1914 has
caused a tremendous revaluation of values and a
constant watching out for the dark forces of life.

Nevertheless, Scriabin's course is one of the most worth while arguments in favour of an acceptance of God's world with its ineffaceable boons : transcendent fancy and divine creation. Not all is wrong with a world where a life complete, noble, intellectually keen, beautiful in form and contents, and above all rich in everlasting joy to humanity, has been lived before our very eyes. Let us rejoice in the heritage left to us by this Messiah among men.

BIBLIOGRAPHY

1. *Musical Contemporary*, vols. 4–5, Dec. 1915 and Jan. 1916 (Petrograd).

2. V. G. Karatuigin, "Scriabin" (Petrograd).

3. Evgeny Gunst, "Scriabin and his Creative Activity" (Moscow, 1915).

4. L. Sabaneiev, "Scriabin" (Moscow, 1916).

5. A. Eaglefield Hull, "Scriabin, a Great Russian Tone-Poet," Library of Music and Musicians (London, 1916).

N.B.—The first four works are in Russian.

NOTE.—"The Handbook to the Piano Works of A. Scriabin," by M. Montagu-Nathan, published by J. & W. Chester, will also be found useful for reference.

LIST OF PUBLISHED WORKS OF
SCRIABIN

Op. 1.	Valse for piano. . . .	ed. Jurgenson,	1893
Op. 2.	3 pieces for piano . . .	do.	1893
Op. 3.	10 Mazurkas for piano .	do.	1893
Op. 4.	Allegro appassionato for piano	ed. Beliaev,	1894
Op. 5.	2 Nocturnes for piano .	ed. Jurgenson,	1893
Op. 6.	1st Sonata for piano . .	ed. Beliaev,	1895
Op. 7.	2 Impromptus à la Mazur for piano	ed. Jurgenson,	1893
Op. 8.	12 Studies for piano . .	ed. Beliaev,	1895
Op. 9.	Prelude and Nocturne for piano	do.	1895
Op. 10.	2 Impromptus for piano .	do.	1895
Op. 11.	24 Preludes for piano. .	do.	1897
Op. 12.	2 Impromptus for piano .	do.	1897
Op. 13.	6 Preludes for piano . .	do.	1897
Op. 14.	2 Impromptus for piano .	do.	1897
Op. 15.	5 Preludes for piano . .	do.	1897
Op. 16.	5 Preludes for piano . .	do.	1897
Op. 17.	7 Preludes for piano . .	do.	1897
Op. 18.	Allegro de Concert for piano	do.	1897
Op. 19.	2nd Sonata for piano . .	do	1898
Op. 20.	Concerto for piano with orchestra	do.	1898
Op. 21.	Polonaise for piano . .	do.	1898
Op. 22.	4 Preludes for piano . .	do.	1898

Op. 23.	3rd Sonata for piano . .	ed. Beliaev, 1898
Op. 24.	Rêverie for orchestra . .	do. 1899
Op. 25.	9 Mazurkas for piano .	do. 1899
Op. 26.	1st Symphony for orchestra and chorus . .	do. 1900
Op. 27.	2 Preludes for piano . .	do. 1901
Op. 28.	Fantasia for piano . . .	do. 1901
Op. 29.	2nd Symphony for orchestra.	do. 1903
Op. 30.	4th Sonata for piano . .	do. 1904
Op. 31.	4 Preludes for piano . .	do. 1904
Op. 32.	2 Poems for piano. . .	do. 1904
Op. 33.	4 Preludes for piano . .	do. 1904
Op. 34.	Tragic Poem for piano .	do. 1904
Op. 35.	3 Preludes for piano . .	do. 1904
Op. 36.	Satanic Poem for piano .	do. 1904
Op. 37.	4 Preludes for piano . .	do. 1904
Op. 38.	Valse for piano. . . .	do. 1904
Op. 39.	4 Preludes for piano . .	do. 1904
Op. 40.	2 Mazurkas for piano .	do. 1904
Op. 41.	Poem for piano. . . .	do. 1904
Op. 42.	8 Studies for piano . .	do. 1904
Op. 43.	3rd Symphony (" Divine Poem ") for orchestra .	do. 1905
Op. 44.	2 Poems for piano. . .	do. 1905
Op. 45.	3 pieces for piano . . .	do. 1905
Op. 46.	Scherzo for piano . . .	do. 1905
Op. 47.	Quasi-valse for piano . .	do. 1905
Op. 48.	4 Preludes for piano . .	do. 1906
Op. 49.	3 pieces for piano . . .	do. 1906
Op. 50.	Never published	
Op. 51.	4 pieces for piano . . .	do. 1907
Op. 52.*	3 pieces for piano . . (Kussevitski's edition)	ed. Russe de Musique, 1911
Op. 53.*	5th Sonata for piano . .	do. 1911

* These two works originally appeared in Scriabin's own edition in 1908.

Op. 54. The Poem of Ecstasy, for
orchestra . . . . . ed. Beliaev, 1908
Op. 55. Never published.
Op. 56. 4 pieces for piano . . . do. 1908
Op. 57. 2 pieces for piano . . . do. 1908
Op. 58. "Feuillet d'album," for ed. Russe de
piano . . . . . . Musique, 1911
(in an album of pieces by Russian composers.)
Op. 59. 2 pieces for piano ed. Russe de Musique, 1913
Op. 60. "Prometheus" (The
Poem of Fire) for or-
chestra and piano with
organ, chorus, and
clavier à lumière . . do. 1913
Op. 61. Poème-Nocturne for
piano . . . . . do. 1913
Op. 62. 6th Sonata for piano . . do. 1912
Op. 63. 2 Poems for piano. . . do. 1913
Op. 64. 7th Sonata for piano . . do. 1912
Op. 65. 3 Studies for piano. . . ed. Jurgenson, 1913
Op. 66. 8th Sonata for piano . . do. 1913
Op. 67. 2 Preludes for piano . . do. 1913
Op. 68. 9th Sonata for piano . . do. 1913
Op. 69. 2 Poems for piano. . . do. 1913
Op. 70. 10th Sonata for piano. . do. 1913
Op. 71. 2 Poems for piano. . . do. 1914
Op. 72. "Vers la flamme" Poem
for piano . . . . . do. 1914
Op. 73. 2 Dances for piano . . do. 1914
Op. 74. 5 Preludes for piano . . do. 1914

INDEX